Talk of the City

Broadcasting House, London, in the late 1930s. With war in Europe looming on the horizon, in light entertainment radio there is the bizarre spectacle of costumed singers and dancers performing live in a medium where they can only be heard and not seen. Robbie, the mercurial Master of Ceremonies of the popular 'Friday Night at Eight', has a playful and devious imagination. Together with radio producer Clive, the two hatch a dangerous and ~~~~~~~ new form of radio broadcast to h~~~~~~~~~~~~~ sinister truth about the devastati~~~~~~~~~~~ Europe.

Stephen Poliakoff, born in 195~~~~~~~~~~~~~~~~~~ ...ter in residence at the National Theatre for 1976 and the same year won the *Evening Standard*'s Most Promising Playwright award for *Hitting Town* and *City Sugar*. He has also won a BAFTA award for the Best Single Play for *Caught on a Train* in 1980 and the *Evening Standard*'s Best British Film award for *Close My Eyes* in 1992. His plays and films include *Clever Soldiers* (1974), *The Carnation Gang* (1974), *Hitting Town* (1975), *City Sugar* (1975), *Heroes* (1975), *Strawberry Fields* (1977), *Stronger than the Sun* (1977), *Shout Across the River* (1978), *American Days* (1979), *The Summer Party* (1980), *Bloody Kids* (1980), *Caught on a Train* (1980), *Favourite Nights* (1981), *Soft Targets* (1982), *Runners* (1983), *Breaking the Silence* (1984), *Coming in to Land* (1987), *Hidden City* (1988), *She's Been Away* (1989), *Playing with Trains* (1989), *Close My Eyes* (1991), *Sienna Red* (1992), *Century* (1994), *Sweet Panic* (1996), *Blinded by the Sun* (1996) and *The Tribe* (1997).

for a complete catalogue of Methuen Drama titles write to:

Methuen
Random House
20 Vauxhall Bridge Road
London SW1V 2SA

Talk of the City

Stephen Poliakoff

Copyright © 1998 by Stephen Poliakoff
The right of Stephen Poliakoff to be identified as the author of this work
has been asserted by him in accordance with the
Copyright, Designs and Patents Act, 1988

First published in Great Britain in 1998
by Methuen
Random House, 20 Vauxhall Bridge Road, London SW1V 2SA

Random House Australia (Pty) Limited
20 Alfred Street, Milsons Point, Sydney, New South Wales 2061, Australia

Random House New Zealand Limited
18 Poland Road, Glenfield, Auckland 10, New Zealand

Random House South Africa (Pty) Limited
Endulini, 5A Jubilee Road, Parktown 2193, South Africa

BBC copyright details appear on p. xxix

Random House UK Limited Reg. No. 954009

A CIP catalogue record for this book is available from the British Library

Papers used by Random House UK Limited are natural, recyclable products
made from wood grown in sustainable forests. The manufacturing processes
conform to the environmental regulations of the country of origin.

ISBN 0 413 72870 6

Typeset by Deltatype Ltd, Birkenhead, Merseyside
Printed and bound in Great Britain by
Mackays of Chatham PLC, Chatham, Kent

Contents

SOME BACKGROUND MATERIAL –
THE BBC IN THE THIRTIES

From Maurice Gorham's Sound and Fury

It was . . . the worst period in its history. The Corporation
was a bit above itself: it had never been so pompous, self-
righteous, and aloof. Between 1932, when it went to
Broadcasting House, and 1938, when Reith left for Imperial
Airways, there were great events that did more than ever to
make it conscious of its position as a public institution, and it
set itself to behave as it thought a public institution ought to
behave . . . Administration had always been a bit of a
stumbling block in the BBC, because Reith and Carpendale
made it unduly strong: I believe they really thought that
everybody who was doing a productive job was necessarily
childish and irresponsible and needed controlling by
somebody who was concerned only with In and Out trays . . .
I always suspected that, as the dons in *Zuleika Dobson* dreamt
of an Oxford unmarred by undergraduates, our BBC
executives dreamt of a BBC untroubled by broadcasts . . .

Although the BBC was so anxious not to let the names of
its staff be known, it had a touching confidence in their
superiority to all outside talent. Whenever programme
standards were being discussed, it was explained that the
various light programmes from outside sources – seaside
concerts and so on – could be greatly improved if only there
were more BBC staff to go and work on them. I was poorly
received when I suggested that the people who ran these
shows probably knew quite a bit about public taste and it did
not follow that the shows would be improved by anybody else
just because he was on the staff of the BBC . . . In
programme-planning circles they talked easily about contracts
and alternatives, this kind of audience and that kind, successes
and failures, good programmes and bad; and it was all based
on what the BBC officials themselves thought, plus various
odd impressions gathered from correspondence (which is a
notoriously unreliable guide), Press comment that nobody in
the BBC is supposed to read or at least to take seriously, and

occasional *obiter dicta* from friends, charwomen, and people met in the train.

Ariel

Ariel, *the BBC's in-house magazine, reflects the character of the organisation. In the 1930s it was characterised by the rather arch tones and heavy-handed humour of a boy's public-school magazine. The issue dated December 1938, a painfully self-conscious spoof of those very magazines, said it all:*

> 'Before we break up for the hols, we should like to congratulate the School on a most promising start to the new school year. In every House there have been signs of unusual activity and although it seemed at one moment as if the Crisis would interfere a bit with Games, it now looks as if all teams are in for a jolly good season. Don't forget, though, that it's not really the number of wins or goals scored that matters, it's The Game . . . The sandbags in the School Hall have at last been removed and our many visitors can see us in all our marble dignity again. Let us see to it that we live up to that dignity and to our reputation as the cleanest players of the game on the air; let us be proud to proclaim ourselves true radio chums of St Ogilvie's . . .'

Talks Department is so Different! (*Ariel*, December 1937)

The members of Talks Department are commonly pictured as a lot of highbrows, painstakingly queer and cranky, and 'different', somewhat aloof from and (in their own estimation) superior to the general run of their colleagues in other departments of the Programme Division . . . Between them they are responsible for arranging and presenting all the talks broadcast in the National and main Regional programmes, so they have to be at least on speaking terms with intellectuality. As to their alleged superiority, it is true that all those who wear any hats at all wear black ones, that almost every assistant is reckoned so important that he has a secretary all to himself, and that they are all perched high up on the fifth floor of Broadcasting House. Against these things, set the fact that their offices are the tiniest and most inconvenient bathing-boxes in the whole of the Corporation.

Director of Talks is Sir Richard Maconachie, white-haired and genial. You can turn him up in *Who's Who* and discover that he was British Minister to Afghanistan from 1930 to 1935. He came to the BBC only last January. His office, void as yet of any personal ornament, is Room 532 and he doesn't leave it more than he can help because he still loses himself in the corridors, habitually turning right when he should turn left . . .

GR Barnes is Assistant Director of talks, in tiny Room 507. Either DT or he reads every word of every script before it is broadcast, including all final alterations up to zero hour. Barnes was educated for the Royal Navy at Osborne and Dartmouth, and returned (unique feat) to Dartmouth as a master, a contemporary with Bill Alford of School Broadcasts. His secretary, Miss Norah Millar, shares Miss Michael's office. She is an ardent violinist.

Christopher Salmon, scarcely ever to be found in his office, Room 503, came to Talks from the West Region two years ago. He plans (far ahead) big, important talks series such as the one on Population (last spring), on Coal (this autumn), and Peace (due in the New Year). A great character at the weekly meeting, where he is apt to express his boredom in a minor strip-tease act – coat, waistcoat, collar etc – but sometimes merely falls fast asleep. Miss Joan Beach, who works for and with him, is a pronounced blonde, who is fond of hiking and rowing. Decorating the window of their joint office are a set of Ambrose-Heal-like patterned curtains, a legacy from JSA Salt, now North regional PD.

Miss Moyra Harper . . . is the golden-haired Harrogate girl introduced in this *Ariel* feature last December when she was in Press Department. She came to Talks six months ago and likes it very much, thank you. She is shared by Guy Burgess, and works with him in Room 506. Burgess is the unofficial 'bright ideas' man of the department, a product of the Staff Training School, of which he was one of the original members. He brightens up the department too, with his dimples, his weird nautical belt, picked up in a marine-store in Aldgate, and the clockwork Donald Duck on his desk . . .

Ian Cox, in Room 509, now looks after science talks and poetry readings . . . He was a member of the Oxford Hudson Straits Arctic Expedition, and still carries an enormous decorative bowie-knife of his own design and manufacture. He is also notorious for designing a unique map of Cambridge, showing all the pubs.

Well, what do you think of them? Are they more human than you imagined?

Ariel *also contained profiles of staff and features like 'Is there a BBC type of feminine beauty?' – a question it answered with photographs of a dozen virtually identical women – and 'A man's views on women' (written by a woman, Elizabeth Mary Barker of News department) and 'A woman's views on men' (written by a man, Max Kester of Variety), which ended: 'We must all, men and women, sit down and talk things over in a spirit of mutual understanding and co-operation, and we shall obliterate the few remaining differences between the sexes in next to no time.' (Ariel, December 1937)*

From the Star, *8 January 1937*
NO JOB FOR YOUNG MEN
'Dead End', And Salaries Not Good Enough
Big changes are taking place in the announcers department of the BBC. Familiar voices will be heard no more; new ones are taking their places. And a chief reason is – dissatisfaction among the younger men over salaries and lack of prospects. They are ambitious and dislike the idea of being at a dead end . . . It now seems likely that when vacancies occur in the announcers' department, older men will be appointed.

From the BBC's Written Archives Centre, 1985
The Position of Women in the BBC
In May 1932 the BBC instituted a policy of not employing married women. The justification was that married women with husbands to support them should not take jobs from single women who had to support themselves, and by October of that year it was clear that marriage for many women in the Corporation would lead to dismissal. There was

an immediate reaction from women's organisations who
believed this to be illegal under the 1919 Sex Disqualification
(Removal) Act. This stated: 'Women shall not be disqualified
by sex or marriage from holding or continuing to hold any
civil employment or position.'

Despite these protests the Marriage Bar became official in
1933. A memorandum was addressed to all women staff
stating 'the retention on the staff of women who marry must
not be taken for granted'. This memorandum had been
drafted many times: the Corporation was conscious of possible
protests and damage to its image as an enlightened employer.
Indeed, when the document was leaked to the press,
subsequent articles accused the BBC of 'Hitlerite action',
prying and behaving like a dictatorship . . . It was assumed
that the work of a married woman 'would suffer due to her
many home duties'. However, the Corporation excepted those
who 'regard themselves equally with their husbands as
workers and not as domestic partners in the marriage'. Also
exempted from the Bar at the other end of the scale were
lavatory attendants and charwomen, because it was 'a normal
custom' for 'women of this class' to have outside employment.
Other women if they wished to continue working for the BBC
after marriage had to go before a Tribunal. Their conclusions
could be rather personal: 'The Tribunal thought Miss
Bawden might be well advised to defer her marriage for two
years . . .'

In 1937 it was suggested that the Marriage Bar should be
relaxed, but instead it was decided that all women below
Grade 'C' should automatically be dismissed on marriage
without the right to appeal to the Tribunal.

Variety

From the BBC Annual, *1937*
Operettas and musical comedy still stand out as the most
elaborate items of the Variety Department's programmes.
Adaptations of pre-War successes are always popular,
particularly among middle-aged listeners, and these listeners
were catered for by broadcasts of *The Gipsy Princess, My Lady*

Frayle (with Edith Day and Cecil Humphreys), *The Arcadians*, *Gipsy Love* (with Heddle Nash) and *Princess Caprice*, which latter production owed no small measure of its success to the fruity witticisms of George Graves, the famous comedian, who was playing his original part. A younger generation welcomed *The Student Prince, Rio Rita, No, No, Nanette* (with Binnie Hale), *Monsieur Beaucaire, La Vie Parisienne* and *The Vagabond King*, in which Bebe Daniels played the leading part.

Entertainment of the revue order was provided by George Robey in *Here's George*, Ronald Frankau and his company in *You Ought to See Us* and Rex London who wrote words and music for *London's Latest*, besides appearing in it himself; while Lauri Wylie, famous as a revue author for the stage, established a radio name with *Wireless Puppets*, two editions of which starred Billy Merson. The popular north country comedian Sandy Powell appeared in three editions of his *Album*; while three late-night revues of the more sophisticated order were broadcast in the late spring and autumn.

Almost in the revue category fall *The White Coons* and *Kentucky Minstrels*. Until this year *The White Coons* had only been a summer feature, but such was their success that it was decided to continue them throughout the winter, alternating them with *Kentucky Minstrels*.

Concert Party was very much to the fore in 1936. During the spring 'The Air-do-Wells' and Greatorex Newman's 'Fol-de-Rols' broadcast regularly from the studio, followed by Clarkson Rose's 'Twinkle'. The summer season witnessed the initiation of a series of outside broadcasts from the seaside resorts. These were organised by Harry S. Pepper in conjunction with Dave Burnaby, and embraced all the leading parties. Perhaps the greatest success – it was certainly the most original idea – was achieved in Bank Holiday week, when an hour's programme was broadcast from the three 'Fol-de-Rols' companies around the coast – at Eastbourne, Hastings and Llandudno – the programme terminating with a burlesque melodrama whose characters were divided between the three parties. Touch was kept by means of headphones and portable receiving sets, and, in this way, Eastbourne, Hastings and Llandudno were on the air at one and the same time. Even the three respective audiences shared the success, since they were called upon to take the part of 'villagers'. Not a hitch marred the experiment . . .

Reminiscence is an ever-welcome offering in radio, so it is not surprising that *Scrapbooks*, presented by Leslie Baily and Charles Brewer, are high in popular favour. These, too, present well-known personalities from every walk of life and the artistic world to the public. *Scrapbooks* for 1924, 1901 and 1908 have been broadcast during 1936, including contributions from the Countess of Oxford and Asquith, Lord Desborough, the Marchese Marconi, Dame Sybil Thorndike and Shaw Desmond . . .

Inspector Hornleigh Investigates (No 48)

Hornleigh (*into phone*)   Hornleigh speaking . . . Yes, sir . . . Where? . . . (*Slowly*.) 27 Sutherland Avenue. Very good, sir. Yes, I'll go down there at once. Thank you very much. (*Replaces receiver. To Bingham*.) Get the car ready, Bingham.

Bingham   What is it this time?

Hornleigh   There's been a burglary at Sir Alfred Wynn's home. They got away with about £2,000 worth of jewels.

Bingham   I'll have the car ready in a minute, sir. (*Fade out. Pause*.)

*

Sir Alfred   You are Inspector Hornleigh, I suppose. The Superintendent told me you were coming down.

Hornleigh   This is Sergeant Bingham, my assistant.

Sir Alfred   How do you do.

Bingham   How do you do, sir.

Sir Alfred   I'm sorry to drag you all this way at this time of night, but I thought that the quicker the police were on the job, the easier it would be for them to find the necessary clues.

Hornleigh   That's right, Sir Alfred. Now will you please tell me what's happened . . .

*

Sir Alfred   Well, Inspector, this is Page, and this is Mrs Thompson.

Mrs Thompson   I don't know nuffin' about it, sir. I swear I don't! I was in bed by 9 o'clock.

Hornleigh   All right! All right! You needn't be afraid, Mrs Thompson. I only want you to answer a few questions. You see, we have got to clear up this case, and I'm sure you will help Sir Alfred in any way you can, to recover his jewels.

Mrs Thompson   Not 'arf, sir! But I tells you, I don't know nuffin'. I sleep like a log. Last year, we had a fire in the 'ouse and I only woke up when the fireman came into me room to rescue me!

Hornleigh (*laughing*)   Well, that seems to be a good proof of a sound sleeper . . .

*

Hornleigh   I think I have cleared the case, Sir Alfred. The person who smashed the window and stole the jewels was . . . (*Fade out.*)

Announcer   Who stole Sir Alfred's jewels? You heard the evidence and the slip the criminal made when he was questioned by Inspector Hornleigh. The solution of this problem will be given later in this programme . . .

Despite the frivolity suggested by all this, however, there were far-sighted producers already experimenting with the idea of the drama-documentary – a controversial form of broadcasting about which debate still rages. In the 1970s the series Holocaust *was much derided in the British press but had an enormous impact in Germany, where people were seeing these events dramatised for the first time on their televisions.*

Abdication: *On the death of King George V in 1936, his son succeeded to the throne as Edward VIII. However, because of his relationship with Mrs Wallis Simpson, an American divorcée whom the law prevented him from marrying, Edward chose to abdicate. In December 1936 the crown passed to his brother George VI and Edward was created Duke of Windsor. He married Mrs Simpson and they lived the rest of their lives in Europe.*

The Power of Radio: *The broadcast on 30 October of an adaptation of HG Wells's* The War of the Worlds *by Orson Welles's Mercury theatre of the Air created panic across America when listeners tuning in mid-broadcast from other stations mistook the realistic on-the-spot reportage of the play for genuine news flashes. It was estimated at the time that of the 32,000,000 families in the United States, 27,500,000 had radios – 'a greater proportion than have telephones, automobiles, plumbing, electricity, newspapers or magazines.'*

Munich Agreement: *In September 1938, in an attempt to avert the crisis caused by Hitler's escalating demands, Prime Minister Neville Chamberlain, the French Prime Minister Daladier and Mussolini went to Munich and signed an Agreement with Hitler sanctioning Germany's annexation of the Sudetenland area of Czechoslovakia, on the understanding that no further territorial demands would be made. Chamberlain returned to London proclaiming 'Peace with honour, peace for our time'. Winston Churchill said 'England has been offered a choice between war and shame. She has chosen shame and will get war.'*

Kristallnacht: *literally 'crystal night' or 'night of broken glass'. In November 1938 the shooting of a German Embassy official in Paris by a 17-year-old Polish Jew provided Goebbels with a pretext for orchestrating 'spontaneous' acts of violence against the Jews. In 24 hours 7,000 Jewish businesses were destroyed, synagogues burned or razed to the ground, and over 100 Jews killed. Another 30,000 were arrested and sent to concentration camps. After this, Jews began to flee.*

The Power of Radio

From Andrew Boyle's Only the Wind Will Listen
Unquestionably the BBC itself paid the penalty for Reith's aloof but unabashed paternalism by pulling too many punches in its staid, and often excessively cautious, approach to the unending problem of enlightening its enormous but often bewildered public. The dangerous undercurrents of international trends, speeding the drift towards a second world war which nobody wanted, were by no means always indicated by the broadcasters.

Hugh Gray in the Listener, *September 1938*
The Spoken Word: Broadcasting and the Crisis
This week as never before during the whole history of
broadcasting the people of this country have listened in for
news and information. Two speeches stand out. They are the
recorded statements of Mr Chamberlain before leaving for
Germany and on his return. In a time of conflicting rumours
and divergent opinions, and in the natural absence of any
comprehensive official statements, they did something which
revealed once more the possibilities of wireless. For that we
must be grateful. But what else are we being given? Certainly
less than we might reasonably have expected. I do not suggest
for one moment that we should ask for news that could not
wisely be given. I do not ask for propaganda or personal
statements. Surely, though, it would be possible to broadcast
even one talk explaining, as simply and as objectively as
possible, the facts about the Czechoslovakian problem. Isn't
this where broadcasting should come to our help at a time
when each individual is called upon to make up his mind on
vital matters, and to come to a decision, the consequences of
which are unpredictable? Five minutes in the street or in the
Tube, listening to people talking are sufficient to show that
the majority are extremely vague about the issues involved in
Czechoslovakia. Harold Nicolson has during the past weeks
made a number of references to the present situation and has
also ventured a certain amount of criticism, but even he has
not attempted the sort of explanation that the man in the
street would like to hear . . . Broadcasting has an important
function to fulfil in the national life in times like these. Unless
it attempts something of the kind it is not fulfilling that
function.

*Internal BBC memo, marked Private and Confidential: From North
Region Director to Controller (Programmes): 5 October 1938*
The BBC and National Defence
I start from the position that the BBC is in times of crisis the
most important public institution in this country. It is more
important even than Parliament, because it deals directly with
the individual citizen, on whom, and on whose opinion, rests
ultimately the decisions of Parliament and the conduct of our
Government. The recent crisis, or rather, I should say, the

past stages of the present crisis, have proved this beyond any doubt. Another thing that has been proved is that the BBC's prestige is unique, since the masses of the people believe that the BBC can speak for the Government, and yet is independent of it. This belief should be carefully noted by us, because it not only gives us great authority, but also throws on us a very special responsibility and exposes us to a special danger. The responsibility I refer to is that of 'playing fair' with the people of this country, being, in fact, truly independent of improper control or coercion by the Government. The danger I refer to is that the Government, knowing now more clearly than ever the power and value of the BBC in times of crisis, may seek to secure control and influence over us such as would prevent us from, as I have put it, 'playing fair' with the people. I am speaking now of the period before war is actually declared. On the declaration of war, of course, we must come under direct Government control.

To my mind one of the most serious features of that phase of the crisis which concluded at Munich was the ignorance of the people of this country and the Empire of much of the essential knowledge they should have had. Even now they know very little of what they ought to know . . . and, had they been in possession of essential knowledge which was denied to them, their action during the last few weeks would have been such as to bring into being a completely different situation in Europe from that which now exists . . .

I say, with a full sense of responsibility and, since I was for over three years Chief News Editor, with a certain authority, that in the past we have not played the part which our duty to the people of this country called upon us to play. We have, in fact, taken part in a conspiracy of silence. I am not saying for a moment that we did this willingly or even knowingly, and most certainly there is not a word of accusation against any individual in what I am saying . . .

I am not for a moment suggesting that the BBC should have a rival foreign policy to that of the Government. In any case that is impossible, and even if it were not impossible it would still be grossly improper and irresponsible. What I mean is that we should make it our duty to get the most authoritative and reputable non-official students of foreign affairs to expose the development of events frankly and fearlessly in our general talks and news talks . . . It is nearly a year ago now since a member of the Government said in my hearing at a private gathering that we should almost certainly be at war with Germany by October 1938 over Czecho–Slovakia. That opinion, as I have said, was made to a private gathering, but the facts on which it was based were known to many people outside official circles. It was known to several of us in Broadcasting House, yet we were not able to let the people of this country know, in any way, that such a contingency was not only possible but was actually almost certain . . . Why was the country not told? . . . How immeasurably more effective [the Home Office's] action would have been, and how immeasurably safer the country would have been had the situation been exposed in all its urgency. It might, probably would, have made all the difference between the surrender to which democracy has submitted and the negotiation of a real peace which would have left Europe secure.

In order still further to drive home my point, I will refer to the series of talks 'The Way of Peace'. Nothing in what I am going to say now must be taken as criticism of a colleague because, of course, the character and scope of those talks were not determined by him. But the fact remains that many people inside the Corporation knew what I have been saying in this memorandum, and yet that series of talks was allowed to play about the academic, idealistic fringes of the subject of war and peace. It bore as much relation to the necessities of the moment as the chatter of elderly spinsters at a Dorcas Society's tea-party bears to the fight of religion against sin. I maintain that at that time what we needed were realistic talks by Liddell Hart, Admiral Richmond, Seton Watson, Harold Nicolson, Voigt, Haldane and others I could mention, telling simply and clearly the decisions which we would certainly have to take in the near future, and the state of our military, economic and other resources in relation to those decisions . . .

To sum up, I maintain that critical developments in our internal, imperial and external relations are now taking place, and will be carried much further in the near future. People of this country will have to take vital decisions sooner or later, decisions on which it may well be the future of civilisation will rest. Certainly the future of this country and the Empire will rest on them. I want the BBC to give the people of this country and the Empire, as far as it is available to us, the knowledge required for correct and, above all, timely decisions. I know that what I have been saying now demands a certain adjustment in our organisation for broadcasting news and talks. It requires important adjustments in our relations with the Government and, above all, it requires resolution and knowledge on the part of us at the BBC. I make a plea for realism in our talks and news, and a determination to keep our people informed of developments at home and abroad, developments which concern them vitally, using that word in its literal meaning.

From the Observer, *17 May 1936*
Issues of the Hour: Is the BBC Too Cautious?
It is rare to find oneself in any company at present in which the talk does not turn sooner or later to the issues of peace and war with which Europe and ourselves are now confronted. The subject has never been less remote from the thoughts of ordinary men and women who do not usually pay much attention to politics. I have heard a good deal of grumbling and some wonder expressed that these preoccupations have been so little reflected in broadcast programmes. Even at 9.30, when a desire for the latest news from Africa or Europe has brought everyone to the loudspeaker, foreign items have occasionally been postponed until relatively late in the bulletin, or broken up and distributed among items of utterly minor importance, like a fishing boat which has come through rough weather, or an accident of no significance at home or abroad. The BBC 'observer' in Geneva and his colleague in Paris have been used fairly often for brief statements. But the Corporation has at times seemed anxious to discourage, even to deprecate, interest in the Italo-Abyssinian, or Italo-League issue, and no

attempt has been made to discuss or explain the problems at stake for the large general public at a popular hour . . . If the BBC shrink from the responsibility of arranging a controversial series of points of view, there is always the alternative of a documentary programme, devised with the help of competent historical authorities, which, as experience has proved, could be vivid and dramatic.

From BBC internal memo: Director Overseas Services to Controller (Programmes): 24 October 1938

Crisis Broadcasts

You will remember that about halfway through the critical period NAR [North American Representative] raised the question of talks from the Continent and you agreed that no action should be taken, especially having regard to the volume of news and talks that we were then putting out from Daventry. As a matter of interest I mentioned the suggestion to Bushnell of the CBC [Canadian Broadcasting Corporation], who was then in London, and he entirely on his own initiative expressed the opinion that such talks could only be of a sensational character, would not contribute anything which would help overseas judgement of the situation, and would, therefore, be undesirable . . .

I am not blindly opposed to broadcasts from the scenes of action, but I think there are times when such broadcasts are liable to be unhelpful, misleading and purely sensational, and therefore not in accordance with the principles which guide our action as a British organisation. Illustrations of a certain type not uncommon in American journalism have helped some newspapers in this country to achieve notoriety and popularity, but *The Times* and other papers have not emulated the example of their more popular contemporaries with a view to their own circulation. Similarly I feel that one of the most important things at issue is how far we can preserve BBC principles if we decide to follow in the wake of the trend of American broadcasting. As you know, we endeavoured to maintain in Empire programmes during the crisis a very full measure of helpful comment, information and news. Whether we succeeded or not is, I suppose, not for us to judge. There was certainly a much greater volume of crisis material in

Empire programmes than was thought suitable for Home
programmes.

From the Picton Gazette, *Ontario*
During the present crisis, when we are bombarded by news
reports from every quarter, it is a relief to sit down and listen
to the clear, restful accents of the BBC news announcer. It
has been remarked that the more tense the situation becomes,
the more calmly and coolly he intones his phrase, as if events
had not yet taken place. That seems to be typical of the
English people. They are not given to excitement or hysteria.

From BBC internal memo: Midland Region Director: *14 October 1938*
Broadcasting and international cooperation
Some months ago Mr Whitworth, the Midlands Feature
Producer, put forward the proposal that the Corporation's
programmes during Armistice Week should contain a number
of major broadcasts based on the theme of international
cooperation . . . To a limited extent, of course, we can
incorporate these suggestions in our own regional
programmes, as in fact we have been doing in the last few
months, by arranging various musical exchanges with the
Continent. For instance, during the height of the recent crisis,
our Children's Hour broadcast an exchange of singing games
between school children in a little Shropshire village at
Claverley and Mardorf, near Marburg, Germany . . . I could
not help feeling most deeply impressed by the implications of
this simple little broadcast. Being in progress as it was at the
very moment at which our Prime Minister was in consultation
with Herr Hitler at Berchtesgaden, it seemed to me to
emphasise perhaps more than anything else could at that
moment the unity of men and the insignificance of political or
racial frontiers . . .

From the Star, *23 October 1936*
JB Priestley on the BBC Talks Department
A recent correspondence I have had throws a clear light on
the BBC . . . I received a letter from the Northern Regional
Studio, asking me if I would broadcast a talk on Repertory
Theatre while I was up North. I said I would.
  I was then informed that a copy of my talk must be in the

hands of the BBC at least a fortnight before the date of broadcasting, and that I must go to the studio to rehearse. 'Otherwise,' I was told, 'the project must be abandoned.'

'The project,' I replied at once, 'is abandoned.' In other words, I was not prepared to accept these arbitrary conditions. To begin with, I cannot see why I should send them a copy of my talk a fortnight in advance of my giving it. I have broadcast in America, over the 'national hook-up', on more important and controversial topics than Repertory Theatres and not been required to give them a sight of my manuscript until a day or two beforehand. I shall not forget in a hurry that famous night in Portland Place, when I was due to talk to all Britain and America, and the BBC mislaid all copies of my script, and would not let me improvise anything, and so kept the whole Anglo-Saxon wireless world silent for fifteen minutes. Then again, when my time is limited, during a brief visit to another part of the country, why should I be compelled to rehearse my talk? It is not as if I were a novice . . . If the BBC lavished money and flattering attention on its lecturers, I could understand this hoity-toity attitude. It could afford to be peremptory . . . Any successful writer who broadcasts here is compensated so poorly for his time and trouble that he is doing somebody a favour by broadcasting at all. Please note how many successful writers figure in the BBC programmes. Now you know why there are so few.

From a speech by Mr Parker in the House of Commons, 29 April 1936
With regard to the question of censorship by Government Departments of programmes by the British Broadcasting Corporation, I understand that in certain cases it may be desirable that some sort of censorship should exist, especially perhaps on foreign affairs, where I think the Foreign Office may quite rightly intervene in talks on foreign policy if they think they might cause international complications. Last summer, however, it was proposed that there should be a series of talks in the autumn rather wider than usual, and that both Fascist and Communist speakers should be worked into a programme and allowed to give their views. Mr Harry Pollitt and Sir Oswald Mosley were selected as the representatives of their points of view, and there were other

speakers representing the more orthodox parties. The Foreign
Office were consulted and they had no objection. Later in the
autumn, however, they suddenly raised objection to the
programme, after it had been published and after the whole
thing had been arranged. They stated that it was possible that
Sir Oswald Mosley might be represented as an Italian
propagandist in this country and that Mr Harry Pollitt might
be represented as a Russian propagandist.

The British Broadcasting Corporation with great care
raised the matter with the two speakers in question as soon as
possible and got guarantees from them that foreign policy
would not be introduced into their talks. Nevertheless the
Foreign Office still objected. The talks were postponed in the
autumn on the ground that the General Election was coming
on, and in the spring the Corporation again raised the
question whether they could not have these talks. The Foreign
Office again intervened and blocked the talks altogether, and
that is the present position.

Broadcasts

*Some Broadcasters, however, did make attempts both to explain the
complexities of the European situation and to alert listeners to the plight of
the Jews in Germany. John Hilton, a Cambridge professor and BBC
broadcaster since 1933, was one of the most prolific and popular radio
personalities. He visited Germany in 1936 and broadcast several talks on
his experiences there, which were reproduced in the* Listener. *However,
despite both the seriousness of the subject and Hilton's undoubtedly
genuine concern, his tone throughout is characteristically amiable, at times
vaguely reminiscent of PG Wodehouse.*

From the Listener, *8 July 1936*
From Blunders in Berlin
I must explain, to those who may not know, that the great
German poet Goethe was pure German, and is therefore still
held in highest esteem; but the German poet Heine was a Jew
and therefore he and all his works are now, in official

German opinion, dirt. His name must not be mentioned, his verses must not be quoted, in that he was a Jew. Well, could you believe it, in the closing words of my closing speech I told that vast assembly – there must have been a thousand people and at least half of them official Nazi Germans – I told them I regretted my poor knowledge of German, but said that of the German I learnt at school two lines stuck in my memory, the two opening lines of the most widely-known poem of the great German poet and philosopher, Goethe . . . and believe it or believe it not, I proceeded to roar out to that vast multitude these two lines:

'Ich weiss nicht was soll es bedeuten,
  Dass ich so traurig bin' . . .

I knew they'd see the joke at once, the joke of having Goethe quoted against them, and I expected a burst of laughter and applause. What I heard was a gasp from every part of the hall. For what do you think I'd done? I'd mixed up Heine and Goethe and I'd actually roared out to that largely Nazi assembly the two best-known lines of the forbidden Jew poet . . . It wasn't till afterwards, as we broke up and I was taken away by some of my new German colleagues to lunch and was stopped at every turn and had my hand shaken that I learned just what it was I had done, and how it had given everybody, including the Nazi Germans, the biggest chortle they had had for many a day. And there is nothing Germany needs at this moment more than a good laugh . . .

You see, what sticks in my throat is the harshness and the cruelty and the brutality with which the Nazis have treated the Jews and all those others who do not see eye to eye with them. I wrapped nothing up. I listened to all that was said in reply. I was reminded, you may be sure, over and over again, of what we English had been guilty of in Ireland and in India. But I was speaking, not as an Englishman, but as one of those in all countries who hate bullying and beating. They were for the most part genuinely unaware of what was going on; they knew only of putting the Jew in his place and of suppressing or converting the communist . . . I know, you may be sure, how difficult it is to tell the false from the true in matters of

economic progress. I know how much must be discounted;
and how much may turn out to be the flush of fever instead of
the flush of health. And still more I know how appallingly
difficult it is to weigh whatever there may be of improved
welfare for the many against the cruelties to the few and their
miseries and sufferings . . .

From More About Germany (15 July 1936)
One of my evenings in Germany I spent with a Jewish family.
I brought them longed-for news, comfort and cheer. I even
brought laughter, for I told them, when doors were shut, of
my Heine-Goethe blunder. But it was a sad house: a house to
make you weep . . . Their children have fled the land and
dare not or may not come back, even to see their parents.
The father and mother cannot leave. So far as I can see they
are destined never to see their beloved children again. They
live, sparingly, awaiting the next visit from policeman or party
official. 'I used to say,' the mother told me, 'we lived from
one day to the next. Now I can only say we live from three to
a quarter-past and from a quarter-past to half-past.' That was
a household that had done no wrong, that had done no hurt,
that on the contrary had enriched the whole realm of
German life and culture. I am not ignorant of the case against
the Jew in Germany; I am not ignorant of the fact that there
is a Jew problem in Germany; I have heard all manner of
fulminations and have tried my utmost to find grains of sense
and reality in the wild and whirling words that pour from
foaming mouths. I can't go into that now. I only say that to
me, having listened and tried to believe and to understand,
this side of Hitler's doctrine, of his movement, and of his rule,
is just horrible. I leave it at that. But I repeat to you what I
said last week. Hatred of a nation because of the brute and
the bully in that nation, is no good. We all have a touch of
the looney and the lout, our share of the brutes and the
bullies. Let those of us who hold by love and kindliness and
tolerance keep on the best of terms, as long as we can – and I
hope that will be for ever – with all that is best in Germany;
and help the best in Germany to prevail over the worst. And
may they do the same by us.

When Hilton died in 1943 he was honoured by many tributes and obituaries, including this from the New Statesman, *4 September 1943*
I am not sure that the importance of the loss of John Hilton has yet been properly appreciated. He was the outstanding practitioner of a new profession which I should call 'public interpreter'. The job of those who enter this profession is both to tell the public what the Government is doing and to inform the Government of the public's response and further needs . . . The BBC will have to look for a substitute. For this job of broadcasting about the real interests of ordinary people in a way that strikes everybody as being fair, friendly and yet authoritative is an essential public service in our new kind of society.

From Humphrey Carpenter's The Envy of the World
[Harman] Grisewood, who moved into Programme Planning in 1936 . . . tells how Ogilvie, the then Director-General, suggested that the Nazis could be persuaded to stop persecuting the Jews if the BBC broadcast 'Beatrice Harrison playing the cello in the woods, so that the nightingale would sing for her' – this was a famous programme at the time. When Grisewood expressed astonishment, Ogilvie replied: 'The Germans are very sentimental about the nightingale; it might persuade them to take a more peaceful view.'

From the Listener, *21 October 1936*
Two Views of the New Germany
This Autumn, the BBC is giving listeners an opportunity of hearing at first-hand both sides of certain problems which, although they are vital to others, we do not comprehend because they are not our own. On October 18 two Germans – one critical, the other a keen supporter of the present regime – gave the reasons for the opinions they hold. The speakers in this series are not experts or authorities, and are not in any sense accredited representatives of the causes with which they sympathise.

Broadcast by Harold Nicolson, 26 September 1938
The Past Week
The events of this past week have been so sensational and have followed each other so rapidly, that when we look back

to last Monday it seems to be separated from us not by seven short days but by a whole epoch of anxious experience. I shall try this evening to take account of different points of view and to put the events into some sort of perspective. Naturally, I can only give you a personal interpretation of the position.

The first thing to get into our heads – and this really is important – is that Herr Hitler has two main objectives in mind. His first objective is to bring the Sudeten Germans within the frontiers of the Reich. His second objective is – as it seems to me – to deprive the Czechoslovak republic of its independence. The aim of the French and British Governments is, it would seem, to give way to him on the first point, and to oppose him on the second. Unless we get this absolutely clear into our heads we cannot understand what is actually happening, or take a fair view of Mr Chamberlain's policy and actions.

The week leading up to the Munich meeting in September 1938 focused the growing anxieties of the nation. In the following weeks the BBC ran a series featuring the thoughts of 'ordinary people' under the title 'Everyman and the Crisis'.

A Farmer

It was during that week – the week preceding the settlement – that I began to wonder how this business of the war was going to affect me. I was carrying on a business of vital national importance and therefore I was exempt from army service if I wished. I had always had a liking for anything in the way of training and discipline, having been a Boy Scout for years and joining the Territorials when I was old enough, resigning with the rank of corporal in the Armoured Car Company. I was 36 years old, 5' 10", weighed over 13 stone and was envied by everyone for my health and strength. On the other hand, I had a happy home and a good business and was at peace with all men. I argued the futility of war. Why should I fight? I kept on saying. Why should I and people like me be dragged in to settle other people's quarrels? . . . I talked the situation over, at work, in the fields, the barn, or the cowstalls, and I felt that, much as I hated the thought, I wanted to kill someone, to vent my spleen on an enemy, whether his cause was just, or mine. It seemed to me now to have become a question of defending the people I loved. My nerves were on edge and I went to the local market on the Tuesday ready to fall in with anything, and amongst some of my friends we talked and talked again about the apparently inevitable end . . . On Wednesday I knew that it was just a matter of time before I should leave it all, my wife and daughter, my father and my farm, which was such a joy to me. Should I ever come back, and if I did should I be maimed and broken, or perhaps blinded? Why should I be going to fight? I couldn't get the question out of my mind, although now that I had made up my mind definitely I was really longing to know one way or the other. Friday came with a ray of hope and on Saturday morning the news spread even to us in the country that a bloodless agreement had been reached, and the tension was over. I felt as if a great weight had been lifted from my shoulders.

A Doctor's Wife

There was nothing to do. Our plans for war had been made; the child had been sent away, the gas masks had been fitted, I had seen my solicitor and destroyed a lot of papers. There was nothing to do but wait. But we were restless, made more so by the fact that we were really facing, as we thought, the probability of war within a few hours. The precautions and so on – all that had been rather like making your will; necessary but not meaning you were going to die tomorrow. Tuesday was something like receiving sentence of death . . . My husband has his principle to which he works; a simple one; the principle that pain is a bad thing. If you can relieve pain, physical or mental, you are doing good, and you needn't look beyond that. And what he was looking at on Tuesday night was the certainty, as we both thought, of an appalling increase in the amount of pain in the world. I said to him: 'Look here, I know how you're feeling. Is it worth it? Is anything worth it? Why don't we go out into the street now and yell for peace at any price? Insist on any sort of peace?' He said no. He'd been thinking, he said, that you could buy even freedom from pain too dear. He's been completely disillusioned by the last war; he had four years of it. But he believed that there were things

worth suffering for . . . The idea of a free England – a place
where you can do and read and think what you like, so long
as you don't annoy your neighbours; the idea of honouring a
moral obligation; he said he would as soon die for those
things as die in the course of time just because his ticker had
run down. I said 'Suppose, after all, it's peace?' He said then:
'If it's the kind of peace I think is likely, we'll quit. We'll take
the American job.' I didn't ask why but I think I know. It was
because the kind of peace he feared would have knocked on
the head the ideas he was willing to suffer for . . . I don't
know yet what sort of a peace it is. But I know he's written to
America. And I'm willing to go.

A Solicitor

I spent my twenty-first birthday throwing bombs in a trench
in France – when I ought to have been at Oxford. I
remember quite a lot about war. I remember particularly that
an Englishman and a German look even more alike after they
have killed each other than they do before. I am still young
enough to do it all again – and now my children are nearly
old enough too. I practise a profession I like and earn more
than I use. And I'm happy. I suppose I have all possible
reasons for not wanting war. All the same I think there are
things worse than war. And I think one of those things
happened at Munich.

*When the first reports of the Holocaust began to filter back to England, a
BBC executive is alleged to have scrawled on an internal memo 'The
Jews always exaggerate . . .'*

A review in the Criterion *magazine (1936) of 'The Yellow Spot: The
outlawing of half a million beings. A collection of facts and documents
relating to three years persecution of German Jews, derived from National
Socialist Sources, very carefully assembled by a group of investigators,
with an introduction by the Bishop of Durham'. This review, although
signed with the curious name 'Belgion Montgomery', was believed by
many to have been written by TS Eliot.*

There should be somebody to point out that this book,
although enjoying a cathedratic blessing, is an attempt to

rouse moral indignation by means of sensationalism. Needless to say, it does not touch on how we might alleviate the situation of those whose misfortunes it describes, still less on why they, amongst all the unfortunates of the world, have a first claim on our compassion and help. Certainly no Englishman or woman would wish to be a German Jew in Germany today, but not only is our title to the moral dictatorship of the world open to question, there is not the least prospect of our being able to exercise it. More particularly it is noticeable that the jacket of the book speaks of the 'extermination' of the Jews in Germany, whereas the title refers to their 'persecution', and as the title page is to the jacket, so are the contents to the title page, especially in the chapter devoted to the ill treatment of Jews in German concentration camps.

Researcher: Harriet St Johnston

All material from *Ariel*, the BBC Annual and all internal BBC memos © BBC and reproduced by courtesy of the BBC Written Archive Centre at Caversham.

Articles reproduced in the *Listener*: 'Broadcasting and the Crisis' © the estate of Huge Gray: 'The Past Week' © the estate of Harold Nicolson: 'Blunders in Berlin' and 'More About Germany' © the estate of John Hilton. The contributions in 'Everyman and the Crisis' were published anonymously. The scripts of 'Inspector Hornleigh Investigates' were written by Hans W Priwin. Whilst every attempt has been made to trace copyright holders this has not always proved possible and the publishers apologise for any inadvertent breach of copyright.

Humphrey Carpenter, *The Envy of the World* (Weidenfeld and Nicolson, 1996).
Andrew Boyle, *Only the Wind Will Listen* (Hutchinson, 1972).
Maurice Gorham, *Sound and Fury* (Percival Marshall & Co., 1948).

Talk of the City

Talk of the City was first performed by the Royal Shakespeare Company at the Swan Theatre, Stratford-upon-Avon, on 22 April 1998. The cast was as follows:

Robbie	David Westhead
Dredge	Sara Markland
Daphne	Diana Kent
Mabs	Julian Curry
Milly Dews	Sian Reeves
Clive	Angus Wright
Honker	Tom Goodman-Hill
Isabel	Kelly Hunter
Bernard	Mark Hadfield
Assistant	Dominic Rowan
Arnos	John Normington
Walt	Rob Edwards
Dancing Girl	Polly Martin
Dancing Girl	Katy Odey
Cameraman	Giles Taylor

Director Stephen Poliakoff
Designer Tim Hatley
Costume Designer Jon Morrell
Lighting Howard Harrison
Sound John A. Leonard
Music and Additional Lyrics Jason Carr
Music Director Michael Tubbs
Assistant Director Matthew Smith
Company Voice Work Andrew Wade *and* Lyn Darnley
Dialect Coach Charmian Hoare
Production Manager Stuart Gibbons
Costume Supervisor Jenny Alden
Stage Manager Jondon
Deputy Stage Manager Janet Gautrey
Assistant Stage Manager Michael Stanislaw

Characters

Robbie
Dredge
Daphne
Mabs
Milly Dews
Clive
Honker
Isabel
Bernard
Assistant
Arnos
Walt
Dancing Girl
Dancing Girl
Cameraman

The play opens in February 1937.

Act One

Scene One

The Radio Show.

The back wall is flecked with Art Deco pieces that can shine at various stages in the play. The floor has a severely beautiful pattern on it, evocative and formal.

The bells. The Big Ben chimes before the news broadcast. We hear a cultured voice, who starts to read the news.

Voice-over 'This is the National Programme. Copyright reserved.'

'Here is the news summary and sports bulletins. They are followed by 'Friday Night at Eight'. You will then hear something about an event in British air travel.'

'The Regency Bill has been read a second time in the House of Lords with an explanation from Lord Halifax that, in accordance with the view expressed, evidence other than purely medical evidence could be considered by those authorised to decide whether a sovereign is incapacitated. Lord Snell, the Leader of the Opposition, and Lord Motterton for the Opposition Liberals gave support to the Bill.'

As this item continues the lights come up. The musicians come on and take their place. Followed by **Dredge** *– a young London woman in her early twenties – and two* **Dancing Girls**, *all three of them are in full showgirl costume. They stand waiting as other news items follow.*

Voice-over 'Barcelona is reported to have been shelled by an unknown vessel today, very little damage was done and when the shore batteries opened fire the vessel went away.'

Mabs *enters, a man in his late fifties, large appearance with a soft* *self-deprecating manner. He is holding a leather binder, and a small yellow suitcase. He stands waiting, taking his position at his microphone. The news continues.*

Voice-over   'The insurgents claimed today to have captured various places near Malaga and to have taken prisoner some thousands of militiamen.'

Robbie *enters, he in his mid thirties, he is dressed in full evening dress, his energetic appearance trapped in his immaculate radio clothes. He is also holding a leather folder. He stands with authority by the microphone.*

Robbie   Turn down the news please . . .

He turns to the musicians.

Gentlemen, I have a new signal, watch, please.

He does a hand signal like a conductor.

It is for a slow dark tempo . . . I'll show it to you once more . . . you too, Dredge . . . I'm calling it the skimmer. (*He grins at* **Dredge** *in her costume.*) You look glorious.

Dredge (*laughs*)   Do I? Pity nobody else can see it, isn't it!

Robbie   But I can. (*He grins.*) Isn't that enough?

The news continues, half heard.

Voice-over   'Herr von Ribbentrop, the German Ambassador, will see Lord Halifax at the Foreign Office tomorrow afternoon. There is no information that this visit will be anything more than the normal call after the Ambassador's absence of some weeks in his own country.'

Daphne *enters, in her thirties, sharp rather strict appearance but with a hint of something more playful underneath.*

Robbie   Seen the new sign?

Daphne   I certainly have . . . in moderation *only* please. Now, (*Tapping his script.*) the words of your Parisian interview with Milly are quite complicated, I hope you've studied them – careful of trips, and no deviation.

Robbie (*smiles*)   Deviation, forbidden! Absolutely.

Daphne (*handing him a folded note*)   But there is a note for you – since I know you love last-minute surprises. Thirty seconds everybody.

Robbie *reading note.*

Daphne   It's rather aggressive, and self-important, isn't it?

Robbie   It certainly is. (*Reading aloud.*) 'I need to see you. Might be able to fit you in on Wednesday.' Who is he? I have never heard of him.

Daphne   He's second or third down from Arnold Grove, Head of the Spoken Word.

Robbie   Oh, he's from 'TALKS'! Of course – explains the deadly tone. (*He looks up.*) Is he here, do you think? Tucked away somewhere up there?

Milly Dews *comes running on to take her position, fragile rather nervous manner, she stands near* **Robbie** *at the microphone.*

Daphne   There you are, Milly. Fifteen seconds everybody. (*Glancing round.*) Mabs, remember.

Mabs   Yes, don't get my pages stuck together this time. My hands are nice and dry today. (*Places yellow suitcase at his feet.*)

Daphne   And the suitcase is the wrong colour (*She smiles.*) I don't like 'wireless lies', you know that. (*As she moves off, to* **Robbie**.) To the back of your mind now . . . the note.

One of the big red lights on the set springs on. They are standing waiting, staring around and up, very respectful, well-behaved and formal, in their evening dress and showgirl costumes as the news swirls around them.

Voice-over   'The House then went on to discuss a resolution by Mr Cartland, Conservative, expressing concern at the danger to the Empire and the nation of a declining population and urging a government enquiry.'

Robbie (*as this is going on*)   Do you see a stranger, Dredge?

Anybody watching?

Mabs   It seems to get longer and longer the news, these days.

The other red light flicks on. **Robbie** *begins to sing, the girls dance when* **Robbie** *makes signs, the whole atmosphere is of people well-practised, at home in their world.*

Robbie (*singing*)   IT'S 'FRIDAY NIGHT AT EIGHT', AND HERE WE ARE AGAIN.

Milly (*singing*)   Here we are again.

Robbie   And these are some of the delights we have in store.

The musicians play, the girls dance. As **Robbie** *alters the tempo with hand signals, there is a sharp dramatic change.*

Robbie (*spoken*)   We have of course Inspector Bonnington of Scotland Yard, with a new mystery to solve. (*Assuming upper-class, understated, throwaway voice.*) So Sergeant Ostler, where are you dragging me off to today?

Mabs (*as Sergeant Ostler*)   Well, sir, news has come in of a baffling murder . . . in Pimlico . . . it's being called 'The Blue Suitcase Murder'.

Robbie (*as Bonnington*)   In Pimlico? Not an area I know particularly well, you sure the local chaps can't handle it?

Mabs (*as Ostler*)   No, they're completely stumped . . . it's definitely a case for the Yard.

Robbie (*as Bonnington*)   'The Blue Suitcase Murder' . . . Sounds a little over-dramatic to me. I suppose we better go over there and nose around.

(*Sings.*) IT'S 'FRIDAY NIGHT AT EIGHT'. AND THESE ARE SOME OF THE DELIGHTS WE HAVE IN STORE.

(*Spoken.*) The girls are dancing, the music changes because we are delighted to welcome back Milly Dews.

Milly   Hello, hello, everyone.

Robbie   Milly, you've been very busy, haven't you?

Milly (*reading from script*)   Very busy, Robbie.

Robbie (*reading*)   You've been to Paris since we last saw you?

Milly (*reading*)   That's right. Wonderful Paris, croissants, a trip down the Seine, and some marvellous music.

She sings a lyric in French.

(*Spoken.*) I brought back a song or two for those at home to enjoy.

Robbie   Milly has been collecting songs like she collects hats. She brings a whiff of the continent to our shows, a taste of WHAT'S ABROAD.

(*Sings.*) It's 'Friday Night at Eight' and these are some of the delights we have in store.

He looks up, makes his hand signals, the music darkens, he speaks with surprising intensity.

And Mr Tudor Baines will be here to give us an extract from his current success here in London, 'Dark Waters'. The scene is a rusty old cargo boat, moored in a dangerous port, bobbing slowly on dark waters. (*The music plays,* **Robbie** *connects with the mystery, with feeling.*) The water is thick with debris, foul smelling and full of secrets. You may wake up still thinking about these chilling events tomorrow morning.

They all sing loudly: 'IT'S FRIDAY NIGHT AT EIGHT AND THESE ARE THE DELIGHTS WE HAVE IN STORE.'

The music continues as **Mabs**, **Dredge**, *the* **Dancing Girls** *and* **Milly** *exit.* **Robbie** *stops the music abruptly with a hand signal, the red lights snap off, the musicians leave, the lights change on stage.*

Robbie *sits in the middle of the stage and starts taking his shoes and socks off.*

Robbie (*muttering intensely to himself*)   The rhythm wasn't right.

Daphne *enters*.

Daphne   A *taste* of the continent. (**Robbie** *looks up*.) It should have been just a taste of the continent, not a *whiff*. And you plopped in that phrase about abroad – it came from nowhere.

Robbie (*smiles*)   Unforgivable.

Daphne   Of course. The approved text is paramount – as you well know.

Robbie (*amused but respectful*)   Don't worry – it will always be paramount.

The **Dancing Girls** *and* **Dredge** *come back on, still in costume but caked with sweat.* **Mabs** *follows them, looking like he's given his all.*

Robbie (*to* **Daphne**)   But what about THE SHOW?

Daphne   The broadcast . . . it was not bad.

Robbie   It's never the show – she always calls it the broadcast!

Daphne   And you should be pleased I do. But there were lapses. The 'Dark Waters' introduction was a little intense.

Robbie   I didn't deviate!

Daphne   No – but you dwelt . . . things got a little disorganised around there –

Clive   I noticed.

They turn. **Clive** *has entered and is standing on the edge of the area. He has sharp features, natural authority and is elegantly dressed. He is in his thirties.*

Robbie   You noticed did you? And who might you be?

Daphne   I think this must be the author of your note, Robbie.

Clive   Clive Lynn-Thomas and yes I sent you a note. I need to see you.

Robbie (*startled by his confident manner*)   You wanted an appointment, did you? We'll have to look in the book and see where I can fit you in (*Indicating* **Daphne** *who's holding a ledger.*) It will be at least a fortnight.

Daphne   At least . . .

Clive   I think it would be much better if it was right now.

Robbie   You do, do you! Well, that's impossible.

Clive (*indicating ledger*)   Then keep looking.

Daphne   The only possibility I can see in the next three weeks, is the day they've asked you to appear on television . . . you know this television enterprise.

Robbie   No, I'm not doing that. Nobody who's anybody appears on that! *But* I have other plans for that time. (**Daphne** *turns page,* **Robbie** *looking at* **Clive.**) I told you it wouldn't be easy . . . (*He moves.*) So what else did you 'notice' while you were up there . . . did you have a good time?

Clive   A good time? No. It's not the expression I'd use.

Dredge   It's not, is it!

Robbie (*dangerous grin*)   I think certain expressions are occurring to *us*, aren't they.
Obviously we don't draw the great stars like those that appear on 'Monday Night at Eight' we all know that – but this was a good show –

Mabs   You must have got wrapped up in Inspector Bonnington's investigation, surely?

Clive (*calmly*)   No, that was embarrassing.

Robbie *turns startled.*

Clive   I've never understood why all wireless detectives have to talk out of the corners of their mouths like that –

and never get excited.

Robbie (*dangerous smile*)   Because that's what they do. And I always get my man, don't I, as you may have noticed.

Dredge (*pugnacious*)   He always gets the murderer.

Robbie (*moving*)   Now I think you've already outstayed your welcome . . . so if you'd excuse us . . .

Clive (*calmly*)   But you do something unique in your show.

Robbie   Unique! Do I? And what is that?

Clive   You have a *medley* at the start telling the audience what is coming up – which nobody else does. A totally novel feature, something unique.
The show itself is mere fluff of course, the usual variety items and Victorian melodrama – and that tedious Bonnington.
But the medley is interesting. You move from light to dark, and you stay on the dark longer than expected, not afraid to linger.
You show an instinctive sense of structure.

They are all staring at him.

Yes really.
I call it 'instinctive', because I have no idea if you realise you are doing it or not. (*He smiles.*) But there we are. (*To* **Daphne**.) Found a time yet?

Robbie   I'm off. It's incredible, isn't it! Can you believe this character! Get him out of here.

He exits.

Daphne   I rather feel you're going to have to *wait* to see us.

She exits with **Mabs**. **Clive** *calmly takes out cigarette case and lights up.*

Dredge (*astonished*)   You can't smoke here. Nobody can smoke in this building. Ever. You know that.

Clive   Don't worry.

Dredge   You mean you're above the rules! Are they all as bad as you in TALKS?

Clive   Oh, most of them are far worse. No they are. (*He smiles at her.*) Hard to believe, I know.

Robbie *re-enters, standing barefoot.*

Robbie   I forgot my shoes.

He walks over slowly to get them.

'Instinctive sense of structure', indeed!

Clive   You may think it's ridiculous. But you do have it.

Robbie *picks up his shoes.*

Clive   You should go and do this television experiment you know.

Robbie   Really? What on earth for?

Clive   Because it'll be interesting. It's a terrible journey of course, miles away in north London, but it can't fail to be worth a look.

Robbie   I can't go.

Clive   Why not?

Robbie   I have things to do – I'm buying an umbrella, for the Coronation.

Clive   The Coronation isn't till May.

Robbie   It's important I'm prepared. I missed the Abdication speech, that great moment. When everybody, the whole nation was sitting round the wireless set. And you know why, why I wasn't listening? Because I had to study my script for my interview with Milly Dews the next day. I had to study for our 'spontaneous' chat. (*He looks at* **Clive**.) Did *you* hear it?

Clive (*smoking*)   Your interview with Milly?

Robbie   No, the Abdication speech.

Clive   Well, I sort of had to . . . I helped draft the speech.

Robbie   You did what!

Clive   I gave my notes to Sir John Reith, and he incorporated them into the text with the King.

Robbie (*truly startled*)   You helped write the speech!?

Clive   I'm afraid so.

Robbie (*recovering*)   Well, no wonder this world here . . . the world of variety is a bit of a shock to you! If that's how you spend your time!

Clive   No, no, no shock. It's been fascinating. (*Moving to exit, he turns.*) And we will definitely have that time together.

Robbie *looks at* **Dredge**.

Dredge   What a snob!

Robbie (*moving*)   Yes . . . he dares give me advice . . . ! Instinctive structure . . . we don't realise what we're doing . . . it's all an accident . . . he gives me instructions! (*He stops in the middle of the stage.*) I'm definitely going to buy the umbrella.

Blackout.

Scene Two

Alexandra Palace.

In the blackout, the screams of a trumpeting young elephant, and the deeper urgent, throaty grunts of a young rhino.

Isabel *standing alone for a second as the sounds fade away. She is in her thirties, fashionably dressed, a witty, unpredictable manner, she is drinking tea out of a badly chipped cup. The floor is sprinkled with animal droppings.*

Upstage the only prop is a single, rather sinister looking original television camera.

Honker, *a very enthusiastic rather innocent man in his mid twenties, comes rushing on with a broom.*

Honker   Just got to get rid of these last traces ... then the smell will go as well (*He starts sweeping the droppings up.*) or at least nobody will know what it is, which is just as good.

Isabel   I rather like the smell. It's most unexpected – like being at the circus.

Honker   Well, you know radio people, they can be a little grand.

Isabel   I certainly do know – and you're right, I'm not sure they're used to performing surrounded by rhino droppings.

Honker (*sweeping dung*)   Rhino *and* elephant droppings in this case.

Isabel   They're late, aren't they?

Honker   Oh, everyone is always late coming here! Which is useful today!

He rushes off to get dustpan.

Isabel (*amused, staring at droppings which are now in a pile*)   I won't offer to do anything – because you seem to have it under control.

Robbie *sweeps in, in good suit, fine new shoes and overcoat.*

Robbie   I'm late. I hate being late.

Isabel   They are pleased about that.

Robbie   The others are just coming. It's miles, it's like travelling to the moon getting here! (*Moving around.*) And I can't believe the smell – that has got to go.

Isabel   They had a baby elephant and a baby rhino here. They both got stuck in the lift apparently, poor things.

Robbie   Snakes, they didn't have any snakes, did they?

Isabel   I believe they had one or two snakes yes.

Robbie   That could be it! I can see the camera staring at a dead snake for half an hour for one of those interludes they're so fond of!
Anyway now show me to our dressing rooms please . . .

Isabel   No. (**Robbie** *turns, surprised.*) I'm sorry I don't work here. I'm a friend of Clive Lynn-Thomas, I'm meeting him here.

Robbie   So there are two of you now! Popping up to watch me perform. (*He looks across at her standing by the droppings.*) You know I never thought I'd meet a friend of Clive's standing next to a pile of dung.

Isabel   You know Clive well?

Robbie   I met him once – for a few minutes.

Isabel (*lightly*)   I see. Well, first impressions are pretty accurate when talking about Clive. (*She smiles.*) But I'm not sure you really know him yet.

Honker *enters, greeting* **Robbie**.

Honker   There you are! Hello, I'm Harry Wallace. People, I'm afraid, call me Honker . . . so feel free . . . (**Robbie** *about to speak.*) It's because I honk out all the time apparently, 'marvellous, marvellous, marvellous'. So . . . (*He gets down on his knees sweeping up dung.*) It's marvellous to see you.

Robbie   It's . . . interesting to be here.

The whole entourage enter. **Dredge**, *and the* **Dancing Girls**, *all three dressed in fur coats, and their finest show costumes.* **Mabs** *is in a splendid coat, top hat and cane as if for a wedding.* **Daphne** *is in her working clothes and holding a large notebook.*

Robbie   We're complete.

Honker *turns and stares at the stunningly dressed group, the women looking gorgeous.*

Honker   What a wonderful sight!

Dredge   We thought so . . . (*Showing off her costume, under her coat.*) we made a real effort.

Honker   It's marvellous to see you. It's a feast . . . for the eyes.
Clearly.
But I just want to say and I say this very reluctantly, and I realise the stupidity of it all, but we can't allow wireless costumes on television. We're not permitted to do that.

Silence.

Isabel   That's idiotic.

Dredge   We can't be seen like this?! We haven't got anything else to wear.

Mabs   It doesn't seem to me, to make total sense . . .

Robbie   But nobody has ever seen them when they dress up on the radio!
These girls have never been seen by anybody.
They're totally unknown, completely fresh. You must make an exception.

Dredge   Nobody has ever seen us dance.

Honker   I know I know, it's senseless. But there's trouble for me if I break these regulations. It's all to do with budgets and departments and money – and other ludicrous things.

Dredge *and the other girls stare back at him.*

Dredge (*very quiet*)   You mean there's no possibility at all that we can be seen?

Honker *is rushing off.*

Daphne (*to* **Robbie**)   I told you they probably couldn't appear. I warned you. *You* can be seen, because you're being yourself.

Robbie (*startled*)   I'm being myself?

Honker *comes back with a small table.*

Honker   But there *are* freedoms here. Other freedoms, I like to think. Our show, 'Trafalgar Square', that's what we call it, has real people. People we found in Trafalgar Square, normal people, like the man who cleans Nelson's Column.
And a typical tourist, a foreigner's impression of London. (*Breezily to* **Robbie**.) You've seen the scripts? They're simple, aren't they. When you read the interviews, look up every other sentence, up down, up down, and look *at* the interviewee. You'll get the knack! Ready? (*He exits.*)

Robbie (*taking scripts out of pocket, nervous laugh*)   Ought to be able to do this, meeting everyday folk, good working-class boy like me.

Dredge, **Mabs**, *the* **Dancing Girls** *and* **Isabel** *move towards exit.*

Dredge   *We* could have appeared as ourselves.

Isabel (*lightly*)   You will. Somewhere. And without the smell.

Daphne *takes* **Robbie**'s *overcoat off and exits.* **Honker** *re-enters with two chairs.*

Honker   It'll soon be seven o'clock. Hang on tight. (*He exits.*)

The lights changing, focus on the small table and the camera.

Robbie   At least I managed to bring my own musicians.

He does his hand signals. Music starts. He moves to table, puts the scripts in front of him. Stands for a second alone.

(*To himself.*) Remember you're appearing as yourself . . .

He sits facing us.

Honker (*voice from above, hushed*)   Ten, marvellous, nine, marvellous, eight, marvellous, seven six five, marvellous, four incredible, three two terrific, one, marvellous. Zero.

His voice booms out as **Robbie** *prepares himself in front of us.*

Ladies and gentlemen we welcome you to the British Broadcasting television service, broadcasting from Alexandra Palace, London, and it is our pleasure to present 'TRAFALGAR SQUARE'.

Robbie *looks up.*

Robbie   Hello I'm . . . (*He hesitates for a second.*) I'm Robbie Penacourt . . . and this is 'Trafalgar Square' . . .

Robbie *does his hand signals, the music drops and changes.*

Honker (*from above*)   Oh dear – I forgot to warn him about his hand signals.

Robbie (*does signal, music stops*)   And the first person we're going to meet this evening is Mr Robin Tucker who is the person that cleans Nelson's Column.

Pause, nobody enters, **Robbie** *glances around at the script.*

I think he cleans Nelson himself, the actual figure of Nelson, right at the top of the column. (*Nobody enters.*)

Honker (*off*)   Go on go on go on. We're having a problem with Tucker. Do the paragraph about where we are.

Robbie   So . . . while we're waiting for Mr Tucker. (*He shuffles papers.*) I'm Robbie Penacourt . . . I'm appearing tonight as myself.

He does hand signal, low music, and finds the right page.

Maybe you'd like to picture where we are, we're in the great crumbling Alexandra Palace, a vast old building of exhibition halls, high above London. (*He improvises.*) And it's absolutely miles from the centre!

Honker (*off*)   Back on to script two . . . we have the next person, script two! Everything is back on track.

Bernard *enters, heads for the table and the pool of light.*

Robbie *holds up his hand very formally and stops* **Bernard**.
Robbie *is shuffling his papers wildly. He stands up, starting the music again with signals, and then beckons to the camera, instinctively responding to the technology.*

Robbie   Bring the camera forward ... closer, closer ... point it at the chair! (*To audience.*) We're having a moment's *Interlude* now, ladies and gentlemen ... THE CHAIR.

He walks up to **Bernard** *in the shadows.* **Bernard** *is a dark-haired, short, good-looking young man in his early twenties.*

Robbie (*lowering his voice*)   Who are you?

Bernard   I'm the Baron Freiher von Brandis.

Robbie   You're the typical tourist? ... I don't think – I don't think I can find your script. For the interview. And it may not look good if we share.

Bernard (*confident, unfazed*)   That's all right, is it not.

He slips his script in his pocket.

We could just try to talk.

Robbie   Without a script? How would we? We wouldn't know what's going to happen ... (*He looks at* **Bernard**.) If we do ... what about?

Bernard   About the city, this great English city that I'm in. That's why I'm here.

Robbie *moves back to table and into light with* **Bernard**.
Robbie *stops the music with signals, sits in chair.*

Robbie   This is the end of the interlude now. You're watching 'Trafalgar Square'.
And now we meet, this is the Baron Frei ... Frei –

Bernard   The Baron Freiher von Brandis.

Robbie   He is a tourist ... a foreign eye (*He looks at* **Bernard**, *smiles.*) and we're trying to talk ... about ... London, the centre of this country and the Empire ... (*Suddenly.*) So was it much grubbier than you expected, when you first saw it?

Bernard (*unfazed*) Yes, it is a dirty city, quite quite dirty, but also, I tell you what I think, it is a great warren, a city afraid to show itself, to declare itself.

Robbie You mean it's full of secrets? That's right, you're right, Baron. (*To audience.*) In fact, in a few weeks, maybe here in 'Trafalgar Square' there will be the secrets of London .. who knows, look out for it! Right here on 'Trafalgar Square'.

Bernard And I will tell you something else, and this is very interesting – the day I arrived, just a few months ago, on a train coming from the white cliffs of Dover, and I'm from Leipzig, a quite dark city at the depth of winter, and it is night now, and I'm looking out of the window of my train, as we enter London – and I couldn't believe my eyes. The whole city is shining! I thought this is the most amazingly bright, well-lit city I've ever seen. All of it is revealed. It is like day!

Robbie (*excited, moving in his seat, jumping in*) I know what you're going to say! I know what's coming! . . . It was the night Crystal Palace burnt down, wasn't it? When it lit up the whole of London as it burnt. Wasn't it?!

Bernard Yes. Correct!

Robbie What an amazing night to arrive, in a foreign city! Your first night fresh from Europe and you're greeted by that!

Bernard Yes, the sky was completely red.

Robbie It was, and you could see everything and everybody so brightly. All the couples out walking arm in arm, or kissing in corners, every nook was lit up! It was so un-English.

He starts music with signal.

Bernard It was a huge night – like Noah's Ark.

Robbie (*to audience*) I wish I could tell you some of the things I saw that night ... saw people do ... things even I had never seen before!

He lifts hand, music louder. He cuts music dead. Lights change,

Robbie *moves around stage incandescent.* **Bernard** *stands.*
Honker *and* **Daphne** *run on.*

Robbie I have never, NEVER ever been so embarrassed ... in my whole life. This is one of the worst moments. I cannot *believe* how amateur this outfit is. (*He moves.*) I make no apologies for being a radio beast ... I will be monstrous. If I have to. That was a disgrace.

Daphne (*trying to calm him*) It wasn't too bad, Robbie – honestly, you survived ... it wasn't *that* embarrassing.

Robbie It was a shambles ... no wonder television is a laughing stock.

Honker It was a roller coaster. Heart-in-the-mouth stuff, I had no idea what was going to come out next.

Robbie It was an outrage.

Clive It was fine.

Clive *is entering with* **Isabel**. *He is calm, elegantly dressed.*

Robbie So you *are* here!

Clive Absolutely. I told you I would be. (*He moves.*) No, it was a shock to hear something so unprepared ... probably the only time that's ever happened, either here or at Broadcasting House.

Daphne That may well be true.

Daphne *makes notes in her large ledger.*

Robbie (*serious*) It really was fine? Are you sure? (*Then turns.*) I don't know why I'm asking him!

Clive Yes – it was like watching a traffic accident.

Robbie (*stops*) What? I thought you said it was OK?

Clive (*calmly continuing*)   In the sense that it's unrepeatable
– that element of surprise . . . it just happened.

Honker   Unrepeatable – an unrepeatable accident. But
worth seeing!

Clive   It had danger.

Isabel (*lightly*)   And what's more hardly anybody is
watching so it doesn't matter what happens here. The rest
of the world couldn't care a hoot.

Honker   Yes, sadly only two thousand people have
televisions . . .

Bernard   Yes – that is what I am thinking. That is why I
enjoyed it so much.

They all turn and look at him.

Robbie   You were very good, Baron, very good indeed. I
couldn't have done it without you.

Bernard   Thank you. Yes I was thinking the following
while it was happening . . .
For one reason or another, because of charitable work my
family is concerned with in Germany, I have been seeing a
lot of refugees over there, aliens, you know how they are
followed and policed and checked up on.
(*He laughs.*) I was thinking – the only place I have felt I
wasn't being watched recently, was just now *on television*!
Yes!
(*He smiles.*)   A very good sense of being free from prying
eyes! (**Robbie** *watches him, carefully intrigued.*)

Clive   The other significant feature of course is – there's
no record. What happens here has already disappeared into
the ether. There's nothing to say it ever took place.

Robbie   Thank God for that!

Honker   Come on, everybody, let's go to the Dive! (*To*
Robbie.) That's where I put your entourage – it's our little
hut, where we're allowed to drink. And drink ourselves *silly*,

(*He grins.*) which is marvellous! Come on, let's celebrate.

Daphne   I'm not sure that's the word I'd use – celebrate the fact that Robbie is still in one piece perhaps. (*As she exits.*) A stiff whisky might be good . . .

Bernard   An excellent idea. (*He follows.*)

Robbie   I will join you.

Bernard *stops. They look at each other.*

Robbie   Don't run away. You were superb.
(*He turns back.*) As for you two . . . there's something a bit sinister about you being here.
What are you up to?

Clive   What are we up to?

Robbie   Yes. That's right . . . Why are you studying me like this?

Isabel (*emollient*)   He has something to put to you –

Clive (*rather grandly*)   Yes. I want you –

Isabel (*softening it*)   He has a request –

Clive   I *want* you to –

Isabel   He would like you –

Clive (*ignoring this*)   I want you to come and work for me.

Robbie (*very startled*)   Work for you?!

Clive   That's correct.

Silence. **Robbie** *staring at* **Clive**.

Robbie   I don't follow. I'm just a song and dance man.

Clive   Precisely. (*Pause.*)

Robbie   I don't understand . . . (*Holds up hand and moves.*) No! I don't want to hear! I'm going to the Dive. Right now! Where I belong!

Blackout.

Scene Three

Broadcasting House.

A young man's voice starts reading in the cultured BBC tone, but a little over-eager.

Voice-over   'In the House of Commons this afternoon the Under Secretary for Foreign Affairs was asked whether he had seen Herr Hitler's recent assurances about the neutrality of Holland and Belgium and whether Germany would be invited to extend these assurances to Czechoslovakia. Lord Cranbourne replied that he did not think that the position resulting from Herr Hitler's statement a week ago was clear enough for him to say anything on the matter.'

We see the **Assistant**, *a young man in his twenties dressed in similar suit to* **Clive**, *modelling his appearance on him. The* **Assistant** *is reading the news sitting on a chair, while* **Clive** *moves around him listening.*

Assistant (*looks up at* **Clive**)   Was that all right?

Clive   It was excellent ... but if you want to sound exactly like the original, you need the slight reassurance in the voice – that everything is all right in the world really, that these great matters are in careful hands.

Assistant   Oh yes of course, I should do that.

Clive (*reassuring tones*)   'The meeting with Herr von Ribbentrop, the German Ambassador, was merely routine ...' or those wonderful words when the old King died ... 'the King's life is moving peacefully towards its close ...'

Assistant   'The King's life is moving peacefully towards its close ...'

Clive   Once more 'the King's life is moving peacefully towards its close ...'

Assistant (*more effortless gravitas*)   'The King's life is moving

peacefully towards its close . . .'
That's nearer, isn't it?

Clive   Yes, it was tinged with the tone, it was good.

Robbie *enters.*

Robbie   Well, I'm here. Don't ask me why.

Clive   I think the other six news items can wait.

Assistant (*jumping up*)   Absolutely, Mr Lynn-Thomas. I
will go back to my normal duties now. That was a very
good observation, thank you.

Robbie   Yes, he's good at observations!

Assistant   I'm sure Arnos will be impressed.

Clive   Arnos?

Assistant   Oh, I mean Mr Grove. You know everybody
calls him *Arnos Grove*, after the stop on the Piccadilly line
(*Embarrassed.*) Sorry, shouldn't have mentioned that. (*Very
respectful.*) Thank you again. (*He exits.*)

Robbie *moving warily, a little closer.*

Clive   My assistant. They are selecting some standby
newsreaders . . . in case of problems . . . he's having a go.

Robbie   Will he have to dress up in the full garb, you
know evening dress, stiff collar, even for the audition?

Clive   Of course . . . (*Watching* **Robbie**.)
It's amazing, isn't it – the way this organisation behaves. It
is only *fifteen* years old, and yet it has become an instant
cathedral of broadcasting, managed to create all this sham
venerability – so people have difficulty remembering a time
when it didn't exist.
In *reality* it is so young, but in spirit –

Robbie   It's never been young?!

Slight pause.

Clive   Good.

Robbie (*grins*) I get a good ... (*Moves.*) I got a good! I've survived the first round.

Clive *looks across at him.*

Clive At the start of any enterprise, between two comparative strangers, this is really one of the most difficult moments – this now ... isn't it?

Robbie Absolutely, I agree.

Clive When one doesn't know each other's tastes, opinions. (*Slight pause.*) If I was to say for instance Henry James is the most compulsive story teller there has ever been, bar none, bar absolute none. Dickens is sentimental claptrap, not fit for grown-up consumption, and J.M.W. Turner couldn't paint for toffees ...
(*He turns.*) What would be your reaction?

Silence.

Robbie (*swallows*) If you were to say that – I'd play for time definitely! (*He moves.*) Obviously.
(*Looks at* **Clive**.) But eventually I'd say – that remark you made, that was the most absolute complete rubbish I've ever heard.

Clive Right. I see. Good.

Robbie Another good ... ? Not quite such a big one.

Pause.

Clive (*fingering the records carefully*) Did you get that recording of my programme ... those records?

Robbie Yes.

Clive Did you listen to them?

Robbie Yes.

Clive Tell me absolutely frankly what you thought ... Holding back nothing.

Robbie I thought, without doubt ... it was the best programme that I'd ever heard about Friesian cows.

Clive *smiles.*

Clive   Good. I'm glad you thought so.

Robbie   If you don't mind me asking – how much time did you spend on it?

Clive   Oh, it was not too bad. About eight and a half months.

Robbie   Eight and a half MONTHS! You're not serious – in that time –

Clive   You've done a thousand medleys, I know. (*He smiles.*) The programme should have been at least twice as long of course.

Robbie   But it was an hour long already!

Clive   It would have been better at about two and a half hours. I would have been able to include all the history. (*Forcefully.*) And listeners *would* have stayed with it. I assure you.

Robbie   Well *I* would have stayed. (*Grins.*) I think.

Clive   But you liked the form? The real farmers, going on location as they say – the shape, beginning with the sound of a calf being born, the dark, surprisingly prolonged section in the slaughterhouse.

Robbie (*amused, but impressed*)   The form was good.

Clive *moves with records over to where gramophone is built into the wall.*

Robbie   Is that more of it there?

Clive   No, (*He smiles.*) something even more interesting. (*He turns having put on record.*) You know I said how little time all this has been here.

The record starts, a woman's voice talking softly. 'I can't remember where it was, or when it was, but it went like this . . .' (She begins to sing a ballad.)

Robbie   Yes. Why is this woman's voice important? Who

is she? Was she here at the beginning? The very start of this place?

Clive No. It doesn't matter who she is – the fact is, she's already dead.
This person here is singing to us, not from beyond the grave, but while she's in her grave.
Until very recently we couldn't hear people's voices after they were dead. Nothing remained. Their sound, their voices, had gone for ever.
And now, in this very building – there is a whole room of the voices of the dead.

Robbie (*moves*) I hadn't thought of it like that.

Clive We tend to forget how quickly we get used to ideas like that. (*He stops the record.*) And now, with the Abdication of the King, which the whole nation – apart from you – listened to. And with the Coronation about to happen –

Robbie (*suddenly*) This is an essay in power you're giving me? . . . Isn't it! An essay in the power of the instrument – It's an *essay*, with demonstrations!

Clive I'm not lecturing you, I hope.

Robbie No, no no. (*Urgent.*) *Tell me why I'm here, Clive!*

Pause.

Clive I had a radical thought while doing the Friesians . . . that project was pure, of course. But –

Robbie Yes?

Clive I had an unprecedented thought for the next project –

Robbie Yes?!

Clive To use somebody from the Variety side, from Light Entertainment, in a 'Talk'. Somebody who can sing and play many parts – to help both dramatise and document the world we're living in. Instead of doing a straightforward documentary or talk, we engage the listener from an unexpected direction.

Robbie That *is* a startling thought! (**Clive** *about to go on.*)
Wait a moment, wait . . . ! (*He moves thinking.*) Variety
colliding with the world of Talks! Me in a documentary!
That is revolutionary!

He looks at **Clive**.

What is the subject?

Clive I thought the subject would be English apples.

Robbie (*stunned*) English apples? Why?

Clive (*breezily*) Evocative subject, moving from orchard to
orchard, there are some wonderful stories behind certain
kinds of apples, there's the Egremont Russet, the Laxton's
Fortune, the Ellison's Orange. We take something seemingly
simple and reveal its mysterious history –
(*He stops.*) Does the principle appeal to you?

Robbie The principle certainly . . . but –

Clive The principle appeals. Good! It will need careful
handling through the bureaucracy here, of course. I will
need to write a very lengthy proposal document.

Robbie Maybe the subject matter . . . we could discuss a
little further? Find an alternative . . . ?

Arnos *enters. A man of about fifty, large blustery manner, but
flashes of beadiness coming through.*

Arnos Clive, just dropping by . . . nothing formal.

Clive (*surprised*) Mr Grove . . .

Arnos (*quick nod in the direction of* **Robbie**, *then back to*
Clive) I wanted to let you know – as soon as I heard –
the paper, the one I asked you to write about the Empire
Service, well, the DG is very pleased, very *pleased* indeed.

Clive (*carefully watching* **Arnos**) That's excellent news . . .

Arnos 'Elegant' and 'incisive' – those were some of the
words being used, I believe. You usually come up trumps,

don't you!
NRD approved too – (*Hearty chuckle.*) not that that's nearly
so important now, of course!

Clive (*sharp smile*) That's very gratifying . . . and all those
reservations *you* had, were those noted and discussed?

Arnos My reservations? . . . (*Blustery laugh.*) They can't
have been very serious, can they – because they've already
slipped the memory!

Now – the Coronation. Got to help me out there, Clive –
what we broadcast surrounding the Coronation . . . many
countries listening, got to be judged perfectly. New task,
new paper!

Clive Fine. I'll start right away.

Arnos Splendid.

*He moves over to radio in wall, switches it on, dance music pours out
of it.*

Just watch this – I want you to watch . . .
It's my party trick at the moment . . . it's made an
impression on everybody I've done it to so far.
Are you listening carefully? . . .
It may not work today, of course.

He slowly starts twiddling the knob on radio.

So you move the dial – through all those squeaks and
bumps . . . never know what they are . . . we're going into
France now, we're in France.

The same dance music pours out.

You see . . . and now we move the dial again – and here
we are, not sure where we go next, I think this is Belgium
. . . and what do we have? . . .

Same dance music pouring out.

And then again with Germany . . . and if we're lucky, if
we're very lucky – (*A snatch of German talk comes out of radio.*
Arnos *disappointed.*) No . . .

A moment later, the same tune, but different arrangement bursts out.
Arnos *turns triumphant.*

There! (*Music playing.*) Isn't that interesting? – the same
music everywhere! It's American of course, the tune –

Robbie   It's called 'Laughing in the Night', (**Arnos** *turns.*)
the tune.

Arnos   Yes. Is it? Who are you? I don't think I know
who you are.

Clive   I'm sorry, I should have –

Robbie   I'm Robbie Penacourt . . . (**Arnos** *looks blank.*)
Robbie Penacourt . . . from 'Friday Night At Eight'.

Arnos   Oh yes of course, of course.

Clive   And this is Arnold Grove.

Arnos   Head of the Spoken Word. Pleased to meet you.
Forgive me not recognising you . . . but this is a very
unusual encounter for me, somebody from the
Entertainment Side.

Robbie   Don't worry about it. (*Grins.*) I'm used to it.

Arnos (*staring at* **Robbie**)   I'm afraid I'm usually out on
Friday nights . . . Occasionally, I catch Inspector
Bonnington, isn't it?
Yes. I think that's good value, not quite as good as
Inspector Hornleigh on Mondays, but you're right on his
tail!
(*Moving off.*) Keep at it, keep it all going . . .

Robbie (*suddenly*)   Can I ask you something?

Arnos *turns, surprised.*

Arnos   Yes. What is it?

Robbie   If Mr Lynn-Thomas here – this is a
revolutionary thought, Mr Grove . . .
But if he was to ask me to perform in a *talk*, to help
dramatise that particular subject, either a historical matter

or something happening now, if I was to sing songs and play people . . . doing voices –

Clive In the documentary – to help people understand the topic.

Robbie To engage them from another direction! Would that be acceptable? In principle?

Silence.

Arnos What a truly extraordinary notion.

Clive It is, yes – but that doesn't make it necessarily unwise.

Arnos It's so radical – it goes beyond the revolutionary.

Robbie That's why it's exciting.

Arnos (*moves*) What would one call it? It's a very complicated idea for the listener, they could get confused between what is proper fact and what is entertainment.

Robbie Depends how one does it! But the principle is not ruled out? (*He smiles.*) Is it?

Arnos It's an amazing proposal. (*He moves.*) I'll have to consider all aspects . . . and of course refer it to CBW – and NRD naturally . . . maybe to KF and RDJ as well. (*To* **Clive**.) Further discussion will follow . . . (*He exits.*)

Robbie He didn't rule it out!

Clive No.

Robbie I hope you don't mind . . . that I did that.

Clive It took me by surprise . . . (*He moves thoughtfully.*) but it was an excellent move.

Robbie I thought I'd cut through everything. Smack him with it, when he was totally unprepared. You *really* don't mind?

Clive (*smiles*) No. It was very bold. You grabbed the chance. I approve.

Blackout.

Scene Four

Nightclub. The Night Out.

In the blackout a news item, then an SOS. First an abroad item delivered laconically, and then a home SOS delivered more urgently.

Dance music playing, as in a fashionable nightclub.

Isabel *in a rich evening gown, sitting on a high stool, holding a drink.* **Robbie** *sitting next to her a little distance between them, on another high stool. He also has a drink and is a little drunk. He is in a dinner jacket, his bow tie askew.*

Robbie   I think he's angry with me. I interfered when I shouldn't have.

Isabel   He doesn't get angry easily . . .

Robbie   Why do I mind? I've only just met this man – and already I seem to want his approval. It's crazy! (*He drinks.*) I DON'T CARE (*He drinks.*) He *forces* you to care what he thinks, doesn't he . . . he even gave me a sort of cultural test – which I failed miserably! . . . And then I found myself worrying about it afterwards, all down the street . . . !

Isabel   The Dickens versus Henry James test?

Robbie   That's the one.

Isabel   He hates Henry James – (*She smiles.*) I expect you passed.

Robbie   Really? He talked to me about *apples* as well.

Isabel   Now that I've never heard him do.

Robbie   And the funny thing is *I'm* from the country. I know all about apples. He thinks I'm a factory worker originally, I'm sure he does . . . with machine oil coming out of my ears. Or a coal miner. All intellectuals think like that – if they know you're working class.

Isabel (*drinking*) When *in fact* you were brought up in a field of cabbages?

Robbie Nearly. Turnips. Near Swaffham, in Norfolk. My parents were farm labourers. As a boy I ran up and down behind them as they worked the fields. (*Holds up hands.*) Horny hands of the soil.

Isabel (*warm, teasing smile*) So you're a peasant really?

Robbie Yes. I'm a bumpkin who came to the big city . . . (*He turns towards the music.*) I hate this tune . . .

He does one of his hand signals, towards the musicians, self-mocking smile.

Isabel You're not on your show now – they're beyond your control.

Robbie I have no influence no, away from my variety studio!

Staring at **Isabel** *in her evening dress.*

And what about you? I know nothing about you?

Isabel I thought you'd never ask!

Robbie (*grins*) Been waiting my chance. What's your relationship with Clive . . . been longing to ask that!

Isabel That's not difficult. I love him.

Robbie Yes. Yes. I thought so.
Are you going to get married?

Isabel Maybe . . . who knows.

Robbie And do you do anything else? I have a feeling you work at something.

Isabel I observe.

Robbie Yes, I'd noticed *that*! I do too – when I remember.

Isabel   No, I observe professionally.
When the King abdicated, various people got very
interested in the reaction of the masses, in 'primitive
reactions' as they were called. In measuring them
scientifically.

Robbie   Primitive reactions – I know all about those!

Isabel   Yes – so they recruited people to conduct surveys,
into what the masses were really thinking – by sitting in
pubs, standing in bus queues, being amongst them at the
races. Mass observation. Noting everything down they saw
and heard. (*She smiles.*) I do that.

Robbie   Wait a minute – you're studying the masses by
sitting in pubs, and listening to what they're saying as they
play darts?!

Isabel   I write down what I see.

Robbie   And then you draw conclusions! From what's
happened in this one pub?! Those are their typical primitive
reactions to such and such a subject? You can't be serious.

Isabel   I just collect evidence, I don't interpret it. (*Smiles.*)
Not yet anyway . . .

Robbie   But *I* might walk into this pub . . . and sing a
burst of one of my medleys. Tell some jokes. What would
that signify?

Isabel (*laughs*)   No, you wouldn't be a very good
subject . . . No.

Robbie   Why not?

Isabel   Because you make these . . . these rather
surprising leaps of thought . . . between subjects.

Robbie   How do you know that isn't typical? I may be a
perfect example of farm labourer's son . . . (*He drinks.*) The
whole thing's rubbish –

Isabel   It's not rubbish to try to work out for the first
time what the mass of people are thinking, rather than just

guessing – or not caring.

Robbie   And all the time you're doing this, you have to blend in – don't you? In each pub, each bus stop . . . (*Staring at her in her splendid dress and her posh manner.*) That must be a little difficult for you.

Clive *enters with a drink, he is also in evening dress.*

Clive   No, she's very good at that . . . she has chameleon-like qualities – (*Touching her briefly.*) – haven't you – that come as a real surprise.

Isabel   There you are . . . (*She smiles.*) Tell Mr Penacourt what I do isn't rubbish.

Clive   It certainly is not . . .

Isabel (*to* **Robbie**)   He's using it for *his work* too.

Clive   Yes . . . she feeds me little pieces from time to time . . . when she picks up something relevant . . . And they're surprisingly interested in it at Broadcasting House –

Isabel   Before, they had absolutely no idea what their listeners thought of their programmes – the mass of the audience – the ones who would never dream of writing letters.

Clive   No, we didn't. (*He smiles.*) But *I* got it right anyway – it seems!

Robbie (*grins, to* **Isabel**)   So you become one of the masses?! (*He mimics in cartoon cockney.*) 'Cor blimey, luverly weather we're 'aving, aren't we, darling!' (*To* **Isabel**.) Come on, do it for me . . . I'd love to see you blending in . . .

Isabel   No, no it's not like that . . . I just give off the right aura. (**Robbie** *smiles.*) No, I huddle, or bend my head, dress right, I don't need to talk.

The music changes, she gets up.

Do you want to dance? Clive doesn't dance.

Robbie   No. I just dance professionally.

He drinks some more, looking at them both.

But I feel I'm being recruited for something. You are spies, the two of you! And you have targeted me ... we should be on a night train, going somewhere, with the blinds drawn! – shouldn't we!

Clive Of course I have recruited you, *(He smiles.)* it goes without saying.

Robbie I shouldn't think he ever gets drunk, does he? *(Facing them.)* The thing is I don't think it can possibly be just English apples, it's not just *apples*.

Clive We'll do the apples first, nice and simple –

Robbie *No.* I'm not that big a fool ... there is something else. You're such a pure practitioner ... eight months on Friesian cows! –
Using somebody like me ... it must be because you can't do whatever it is you want to do *any other way*.

He gets up.

Oh, let it be more, Clive ... I want it to be more ...

He moves to the music, dancing with **Isabel***, but not holding her close.*

I'm not dancing ... not in front of him ... this isn't dancing. Let it be about America – because I know America well. Never been there but I think about America all the time ... let it be about America, Clive! You've been there lots, haven't you?

Clive Yes ... I have paid fairly frequent visits. In fact I wrote one of my first reports there on the harmful effects of advertising on broadcasting.

Robbie I can see you striding around New York, lecturing the Americans! Telling them 'you're too commercial'! *(He turns.)* What is our *real* mission, Clive?

Dance music playing, **Clive** *calmly lights a cigarette.*

Clive How much have you been following, week by

week, what's going on in Europe?

Robbie Oh no – please. Not *that*. . . ! (*He moves.*) First apples, now this!

Clive Answer my question – how much have you been following?

Robbie Well, I open a newspaper from time to time . . . and occasionally I glance at the bits about abroad.

Isabel That's more than most do.

Robbie And anyway Herr Hitler is too easy to do, everybody can do him. Admittedly he is not portrayed on the wireless – but you just have to click your heels and scream. (*Grins.*) No challenge for somebody with instinctive structure!

Music playing.

Clive And tell me – what about what's happening to the Jews there? In Germany?

Robbie (*puzzled where this is leading*) The Jews? Well, there are some restrictions, aren't there, temporary things going on . . . because of the rebuilding of Germany.

Pause.

Clive *So – this is our project.*
We will follow a day in the lift of a Jewish man, a real day, a real man, though his name is changed. This is who you will be, Robbie.
He is middle class, respectable, a lawyer, once a pillar of the community, who has also written some rather beautiful songs. We will follow him during a 'normal day' and see how many normal things he is prevented from doing, how many things we accept as our right have been taken away from him.
And at the end of the day he is arrested. His liberty is taken away. You will portray this man and sing his songs.

Robbie (*very disappointed*) No, Clive, no – that's absolutely out! Nobody will listen to something like that for a start –

Clive   They will. This is how to make them listen . . .

Robbie   They want to forget about any difficulties out there! And *I* don't want to be involved in politics either. I'm not allowed to associate myself with that. I *knew* this would start to happen, the spinning of a leftist web, communism, you'll have me fighting in Spain soon, and not just on the radio!

Isabel   Neither of us are communists, Robbie, that isn't the issue.

Clive (*to* **Robbie**)   Stop jumping to conclusions –

Robbie   You're the one who's jumping to conclusions . . . We don't *really* know what's going on in Germany, do we, we don't! And all their attitudes are different there, anyway, and we can't *tell* them what to do, can we?! It's not for us to lecture them . . .
And we certainly don't want to annoy them – . . . the whole idea is preposterous.

Clive   You're contradicting yourself, Robbie – you wanted the project to be much much more than apples, and now you're running away from it.

Isabel   Leave this to another time, Clive, send Robbie your notes to look at and –

Robbie (*suddenly*)   Anyway, there *are* a lot of powerful Jews, aren't there?! That's undeniable.
Maybe the balance does need correcting.

Clive   That is unworthy of you.
You're disappointing me now, Mr Penacourt.

Robbie   Oh, I am, am I!
Now we're going to get the full sneering superiority act, are we?!
I'm sorry I've had about all I can take from you, I have been patronised from the first moment – informed I do my work by accident, *despite myself*!
I'm encouraged to make a fool of myself on that television experiment, because *you're* interested.

Isabel   That was worth it, wasn't it, Robbie?

Robbie (*looking at both of them*)   Everything is so clear to you two, isn't it?! – So blindingly obvious . . . with your surveys, and all the time you have to spare on just one topic . . . Well, *I* don't have that time, and I DON'T CARE IF I DISAPPOINT.

Clive   But I do.

Robbie   What does that mean – that's meaningless . . . You care if I disappoint you – that's A LIE.
I'm just a crude entertainer, a compere, who sings a bit and dances a bit, and has *everything* written for him. That's me. . . ! And he *doesn't care*.
And now I'm off. The useful clown, that you found, that you picked for your own purposes, is scampering off – to the rest of his life!
Which is looking pretty good at the moment . . . Pretty bloody good!

Blackout.

Scene Five

The Walk to the Station.

Robbie *entwined with* **Bernard** *in the shadow, in each other's arms. A lovers' embrace.*

The sound of taxis and distant train doors slamming, as if from a mainline station. During this scene the sound of trains and whistles growing gradually louder and louder, until they completely surround us.

Robbie   You really have to go?

Bernard   Yes. I must go. (*Pushing* **Robbie** *gently away.*) We will be seen.

Robbie   We're saying goodbye . . . and you're a foreigner – so a little over-enthusiasm is permissible. (*He mimics.*) Johnny foreigners are allowed to kiss.

Bernard   And the streets are dark!

Robbie   Unlike your first day here.

Bernard   And the subject of our great debut conversation on the television . . . no script, no censor!

Robbie   We should become a double act – have our own programme . . . (*He is close to* **Bernard**, *gently.*) Only a few nights together . . . and I feel such pain that you're going, I'd do anything to delay the moment!

Bernard   I have to go back – my life is there.

Robbie   Yes, I know. (*He moves.*) In these last few minutes, Bernard – you must tell me what to do about Clive. (*Mimics.*) Clive Lynn-Thomas.
I can't get rid of him, he is pushing and pushing at me . . . attacking my confidence all the time.
But there's something so challenging about him as well. And he has such different values, he doesn't care about my show, what stars are on it . . . (*Suddenly.*) Which reminds me, I haven't heard if the Silver Minstrels are going to be on on Friday . . .

Bernard (*with feeling*)   To hell with the Silver Minstrels!

Robbie   You're right. Here you are, going in a few minutes, and I'm talking about the Silver Minstrels!

Pause for a second; as **Robbie** *looks at* **Bernard**, *the sound of the trains and the platform whistles become louder.*

This is a shocking time to ask such a question . . . but it is the sort of thing you often can only ask when somebody is about to leave. Not that I've ever asked a question like this before –

Bernard   What is it, Robbie?

Robbie   The Baron Freiher von Brandis . . . it's such a fantastic name . . .

Bernard   It's like something from the book, *The Prisoner of Zenda* . . . I know.

Robbie Is it your real name? Are *you* the Baron Freiher von Brandis?

Bernard No. I'd like to say it's half my real name . . . but it isn't.
When I arrived at Woburn House, you know, where most aliens report in London, so many people were passing themselves off to each other with titles and funny names, I did so too.
It's very useful for getting invited to parties, all sorts of things.

Robbie You're Jewish, aren't you?

Bernard Yes. (*Smiles.*) That's correct.

Robbie I thought so . . . I knew it. (*He looks at* **Bernard**.) It's awful to ask this now too –

Bernard Better to ask it, than to think about it after I've gone.

Robbie How difficult are things for Jewish people, in Germany now?

Bernard There are problems, of course there are. It isn't good.
I find it a difficult question to answer in this country. Because a few people ask you . . . and you start to tell them – and you quickly realise they really don't want to know . . . perhaps only half a sentence at the most . . .

Robbie Yes, I know. I suppose I'm like that . . .

Bernard I tell you – I went to a very grand wedding in Buckinghamshire, with lots of people with names like Farquhar-Buzzard and Babbington-Semple, being a Baron was really useful, as you can imagine – 'You must know the von Stauffenbergs?' people kept asking me – And somebody remarks at this wedding 'We must really stop the Jews complaining so much, they've got to stop causing problems.' So you see . . . one has to be careful.

Robbie I wish I'd been with you at this wedding. (*He*

mimics in upper-class twit voice.) As you passed yourself off as a Baron to the Mallenby-Deeleys – Erskine-Mars.

Bernard   Yes, you would have been very interested. There was an Italian waiter who shouted at all these upper-class guests (*He mimics Italian accent.*) 'You're taking the wrong plate! Stop it at once! *Stupido*! I'm telling you get in the queue and wait for your strawberries.' They were terrified of him! I wanted to support him, to shout out, 'Go on, get after them!'

Robbie   I love the idea.

Bernard   *You* were on the wireless, yes, (**Robbie** *turns.*) the night before, I was staying in this big house and they switched on the wireless and there you were.

Robbie   I was! That's a wonderful picture! All of them listening to me . . .

Bernard   But they switched you off – and went out.

Robbie (*loud*)   I really must get off Friday nights! Everybody goes out . . . ! If I was on Monday nights, I'd be coming out of every window, in every street.

Loud, piercing platform whistles.

Robbie   I'm sorry – I'm being incredibly self-centred . . . absorbed in my show.

Another loud whistle.

Bernard   So – this is goodbye then. We keep it short?

Robbie   Yes.

Bernard   Stations are terrible places, people very upset everywhere . . . all these awful feelings of leaving.

Loud sounds.

Robbie   Yes, these trains going to the continent – going somewhere dark. Going somewhere foreign.

Bernard   If we could take a train, you and I, somewhere else . . . ! Completely away from everything, a fantastical city, a tropical place.

Robbie   We will. We will. (*He grins.*) We'll go to Bexhill, we can! I know a special little hideaway hotel, where no one can find us.

Bernard   Bexhill? (*Warm smile.*) It sounds a good place. So just like this – I say goodbye and go.

He goes.

Robbie   Goodbye . . .

As **Bernard** *walks into shadow,* **Robbie** *suddenly yells after him.*

Bernard – don't go.
It's wrong for you to go.

Bernard *turns.* **Robbie** *continues to shout.*

Robbie   I don't care who's watching! This isn't the right time! You're *not* leaving.

As the whistles blow, **Robbie** *calls powerfully.*

You're not going. You're not. You're not!

Blackout.

Scene Six

Broadcasting House.

Clock ticking, after the shrill sound of the whistles. **Assistant** *and* **Clive** *high up together above the main set.*

Assistant (*very nervous*)   'This is the National Programme, copyright reserved . . .' Just clearing my throat.

Clive   It will be all right, just a few slow deep breaths.

Assistant   I can't believe this has happened already, I've only just got the standby job, and now here I am . . . and all those people listening . . .

Clive   They just hear the news, they don't see a face.

That reassuring voice is what matters, be careful not to get too involved, that's all, too urgent – they don't want any immediacy. You're going into their living-rooms, they may even be eating . . . they're used to the news being something far away.

Assistant   That's right. I know . . . you think I can do it?

Clive   Of course you can.

Assistant   I will always be grateful for this, Mr Lynn-Thomas. I shan't forget it.

Red light flicks on, high above the main stage. **Assistant** *now alone, starts reading the news in perfect young BBC voice.*

Assistant   'This is the National Programme copyright reserved. Here is the news summary and sports bulletins. They are followed by 'Friday Night at Eight', and then you will hear some stories of sea dogs, and land dogs. Important changes in the German Cabinet are announced tonight, they affect principally two departments, that of War and Foreign Affairs.'

On stage **Mabs**, **Dredge** *and the* **Dancing Girls** *stand waiting.* **Daphne** *and* **Robbie** *close to each other downstage.*

Robbie   Promise me you are not upset.

Daphne   Why should I be upset?

Robbie   Because I talked to *him*, I discussed things with him, without you present.

Daphne   Why shouldn't you discuss things with him? He is a very rude man – but he's also highly intelligent and interesting.

Robbie   There's no *question* of me working with him . . . spending days and days with him.

Daphne   Well, I guessed you might feel like that.

Robbie   And there's *absolutely* no question of me ever discussing things with him again – without you being there.

Daphne   That's good. That's reassuring.

Robbie   We're a partnership. You are the structure of my whole life. (*Holding her, warm smile.*) Aren't you, Daphne?! . . . A partnership made in broadcasting heaven.

Daphne (*warm laugh*)   Speak for yourself! But I'm glad there will be no secrets between us. Nothing going on behind my back . . . Everything involving us will be completely honest . . . ?

Robbie   No secrets, ever. I swear –

Milly *comes running on.*

Daphne   Enough chinwagging, forty-five seconds everybody! (*She exits.*)

Robbie (*indicating* **Dredge** *and the* **Dancing Girls**)   Don't they look beautiful?

Dredge   We always look beautiful! Fat lot of good it does.

Robbie (*grins*)   People can sense it, I'm sure, they can feel you breathing, you *exude* through the air. (*To* **Dredge**, *softly.*) And I'm feeling good . . . my friend is staying for the Coronation.

Mabs (*studying his script*)   Inspector Bonnington is going to Windsor Great Park today . . . to solve the Gravel Path murder. And Sergeant Ostler goes fishing . . . (*He mimics Bonnington.*) 'Windsor Great Park, not an area I know particularly well . . . why can't the local chaps see to it, Ostler.'
(*To* **Robbie**.) I catch two brown trout – and have to cook them for you! . . . And you are jolly polite to a duke . . .

Assistant (*reading the news above them*)   'In an important speech in the Czechoslovak Parliament today, the Prime Minister Hodza refers to Herr Hitler's speech and to that of Field Marshall Goering's . . .

Milly (*looking up from her script*)   So it's Amsterdam today. And my tulip song!

Robbie (*listening to the news*) His protégé is reading the news, and I'm going to be talking to Milly about *tulips*!

Milly (*twittering on*) I've had an approach, I have to tell you, from 'Monday Night at Eight'. You wouldn't mind me going on there, would you?
Of course it's a great honour to be on your show, but *they* have a hook up to America once every six months . . . if it was one of those shows, I couldn't turn it down – not broadcasting to America!

Robbie You *must* accept, Milly, of course. (*To himself wistfully.*) A hook up to America . . .

The red light goes on, the music intro starts.

(*Suddenly.*) What if we tear up this tulip chatter, and talk about something completely different, Milly, just see what happens. Where the mood takes us?

Milly Don't play jokes like that, Robbie, please.

The other red light flicks on.

Robbie (*sings*) It's 'Friday Night at Eight', and these are the delights we have in store.
Milly Dews is here again.

Milly (*reading*) Hello, everyone. Hello, I'm back again from my travels.

Robbie (*improvising*) Could be the last time, folks, Milly is here! (**Milly** *looks startled,* **Robbie** *back on script.*) You've been to Amsterdam among the canals and the tulips?

Milly (*reading*) Well, Robbie, I was singing, if not in the tulips, then about the tulips. Red, red tulips.

She bursts into a couple of lines of the tulip song.

That's just one of the songs I brought back – for all of you – from old Amsterdam!

Blackout. **Milly** *continues to sing the tulip song during the scene change.*

Scene Seven

Alexandra Palace.

The sound of shrieking tropical birds, **Honker** *with dustpan and brush, a scattering of feathers on the stage.* **Robbie** *holding large roll of paper, and* **Daphne** *her ledger.*

Honker   You don't mind doing the show with the birds? They are a little noisy . . .

Robbie   No, no, it's fine.

Honker   We've had dozens of stories about pigeons on 'Trafalgar Square' . . . so I went a little wild and booked these gorgeous tropical birds instead – very bold I know – but it's justified because the man who owns them, sometimes goes to Trafalgar Square.
(*He looks at* **Robbie**.) It's marvellous you came back – so few people ever come back.

Robbie   No, it feels good being here. So there was no reaction at all to my first television appearance?

Honker   None at all, not a single letter.

Daphne   I told you, you shouldn't ask.

Clive *and* **Isabel** *enter.*

Honker   One day it will be different – if we last that long!

Robbie   *Both* of you – that's good!

Clive (*formidable, cold*)   So – we answered your call . . . Though I don't know why you wanted us to meet here . . . (*Looking at* **Honker**.) Are you still in Trafalgar Square – or has the show moved on?

Honker   Afraid that's where we still are – but it's buzzing, 'Trafalgar Square' is buzzing . . . (*He moves to go.*) Just one word, Mr Penacourt, please don't take this wrong, but those marvellous hand signals you do to the musicians, so expressive, but remember they're not quite right for television – in case somebody's watching, they might see them!

He exits. Pause.

Clive (*to* **Robbie**)   So what is it?

Robbie   I have something important to say ... And we can speak openly in front of Daphne –

Daphne (*lightly*)   I'm just here as Robbie's keeper.

Isabel (*moving*)   And it's *good* to be here because there's a strange sense of freedom, isn't there! Like one can say anything, do anything.
Maybe we'll all suddenly start 'speaking in tongues' – feel energised to pour all sorts of things out.

Robbie   That's right. Nobody watching, no supervision!

Clive   So what do *you* want to pour out, Robbie?

Robbie   Well, about your proposal – I can not agree to being party to any propaganda – but –

Clive (*sharp*)   This is not propaganda for a start. Dr Goebbels defines propaganda as creative energy emanating from one central will – by which he means, loud lies working to one end. *We* are talking about the exact opposite – we're going to demonstrate a truth, using very quiet and simple means.

Robbie   Just wait! OK! (*He moves.*) I'm not agreeing to your project –

Clive   You're not? So I might as well leave –

Robbie   But I don't think I did myself justice when we spoke before.
I've been doing some reading, articles about abroad, and I feel –

Isabel   There aren't very many good reports on what's happening.

Robbie   No, but I read enough to realise ... I don't

think my response was adequate.

Clive   So what are you prepared to do about it, Robbie
. . . are you going to work with me or not?

Robbie   I'm prepared to offer you a deal.

Clive   A deal?! It's not a word I tend to use.

Isabel   I don't think he's talking about a showbiz sort of
deal, are you?

Robbie   The deal is – that we continue to discuss the
project in secret, between us four, suggesting ideas,
preparing carefully, before we approach the authorities.

Clive   Everything I do is prepared carefully.

Robbie *unrolls blank wallpaper on to floor, putting chair at one
end, his shoes at the other, so it's stretched out taut.*

Clive   He's taking his shoes off again.

Robbie   We can splash down ideas on this, where we can
all see them.

Isabel   You want to write that big?!

Robbie   This way nothing is confidential . . .
For instance – I was thinking, Clive, maybe something
more dynamic than what you suggested, something people
can't easily forget. Like . . . when we think of Germany and
Austria – what immediately comes to mind?

Isabel   Lederhosen . . . mountains . . . strudel and waltzes.

Robbie   Yes. And lakes . . . I thought if your Jews, your
Jewish lawyer and his family are on a boat on a lake . . . A
happy scene, a holiday scene, laughter. Suddenly they're
being stoned from the bank, the boat goes round and
round and round, in frightening circles, the stones keep
coming, keep hitting.
(*He is moving in his stockinged feet on the wallpaper.*) The children
are terrified, the boat capsizes, they are screaming . . .
people would have to respond to that! To their cries! They

wouldn't forget that.

He looks up for their reaction, the paper is all crunched up.

Robbie What do you think?

Isabel That's horribly vivid – God forbid that it gets as bad as that. (*Quiet.*) Let's pray that doesn't happen.

Honker *rushes in, to* **Daphne**.

Honker There's a phone call for you – urgent – from Broadcasting House.

Daphne *and* **Honker** *exit.*

Robbie (*looking at* **Clive**) He doesn't approve . . .

Clive No. I don't disapprove. It was graphic. It has all your directness, with a slight touch of the surrealism you like. But we must remain truthful, and factually based, if we are going to be allowed to broadcast.

Daphne *re-enters.*

Robbie What's happened – what's the matter?

Daphne (*quiet*) It's some very good news.

Robbie Don't say it like that! I thought there'd been a death. What is it?

Daphne Something's happened with 'Monday Night at Eight' – *we* have been given the hook-up to America. This Friday.

Robbie Oh my God! Really!
But we're totally unprepared . . .
I need some stars to broadcast to America . . .
I have no stars and no time to get any . . . nobody's ever heard of *me* over there.
(*Automatically turning to* **Clive**.) What do I do, Clive?

Clive You should be asking Daphne.

Daphne No no, no, it's fine, honestly, I'd like to hear your advice.

Robbie Tell me, Clive, please.

Clive (*calmly*) Just go ahead . . . you don't need stars. Do what you normally do – but with a lot more spontaneity . . . break free of the formula.

Robbie I will fall flat on my face then!

Clive No. You won't. And what's more, the more exposure you get now – the better it is for when we make a move.

Blackout.

Scene Eight

Broadcasting House.

The music playing, the girls dancing, they are in their everyday clothes. **Daphne** *is close to them, calling out to them. Downstage* **Robbie** *is watching them,* **Isabel** *sitting across from him.*

Daphne (*to* **Dredge**) Come on stronger, stronger. This is for America. For the U S of A.

Dredge (*as she dances to* **Robbie**) They're going to sense this, are they! Able to *feel* us on air, right behind you, Mr Penacourt, during the show – *exuding.* Going to feel waves of us, are they?!

Robbie Undoubtedly (*Grins.*) *I* can certainly feel it from over here. (*Watching her.*) The Coronation could have done with a bit of you, couldn't it!

Isabel Maybe they can do all the dances that people disapprove of at the moment . . . dancing to jazz music . . . suggestive movements . . .
(*Smiles.*) Forbidden dances on the wireless – that's a good idea, isn't it!

Dredge Oh yes – we could hot it up.

She moves sensually, doing one of **Robbie**'s *hand movements to quicken the tempo of the music.*

Daphne   Susan, stop that! *At once*!
One never knows who's about to walk in here.

Dredge *tones it down a bit.*

Robbie *(watching the girls dance)*   This is why I first tried to
become an actor – what better reason could one have!

Daphne   Right, we'd better move on.

Robbie *looks across to* **Isabel**, *as the girls move to slower music.*

Robbie *You* know all the current dances, don't you,
because of your observing?

Isabel   Absolutely. I've just been to Blackpool to do a
survey on lovers.

Robbie *laughs.* **Isabel** *smiles.*

Isabel   No I'm serious, that really is what I was asked to
do! It's called 'Sex in Blackpool' – I'm walking along the
front staring at couples, counting the times they hold hands,
seeing if there are any couples I can find that are fully
entwined, or are they just sitting very close . . .

Robbie *(watching her)*   And when you find them fully
entwined, what do you do?

Isabel   Just stare, and wait *(She smiles.)* and make notes.

Robbie *(suddenly)*   We should have Sex on the Wireless,
Daphne! . . . late at night . . . for the bedroom – help
people get in the mood!

Daphne *(cutting the music)*   You'll have to have the biggest
wireless triumph there's ever been tomorrow night – to
stand any chance of even the sound of a kiss . . .
(She moves.) Any kiss is still impossible . . .

Claps her hands.

Now everybody, attention, we've some extra bells and other
sound effects. For instance, the bells for the sleigh ride
through the winter forests . . . give us a shimmer of those

bells, Susan.

The bells and other odd-looking objects that make the sounds are hanging on the side wall. **Dredge** *lets the sleigh bells ring.*

And we have horses too, and trains, we have distant ships.

Clive *enters with* **Mabs**. *Both have obviously been drinking.* **Clive**'s *manner is flowing more freely, rather than out of control.* **Mabs** *is merry.*

Clive   Haven't you broken yet, boys and girls?

Mabs   I've been giving myself plenty of Dutch courage. To cope with all this change!

Robbie   Good Lord, Clive – you're not *drunk*, are you?!

Robbie *is astonished at* **Clive**'s *expansive manner.*

Isabel   He never gets drunk.

Clive   I responded to your challenge, Robbie. To see what would happen . . . it's an experiment.

Daphne   Mabs, really! . . . And you, Mr Lynn-Thomas, you mustn't be seen drunk here, it could have serious consequences.

Clive   Absolute balls. Nobody will be able to tell the difference. I'm rather disappointed at how in control I am.

He sits centre stage. Takes out cigarette case, smiles.

Do I think even more clearly or slightly less clearly, in this state? That is the question.

Daphne   No smoking either please – you could be banned from the premises for good. Instant dismissal.

Clive (*dangerous grin*)   I don't think that's going to happen. Who's going to evict *me* from this great building?

Takes a drag on his cigarette.

You know walking here, for some funny reason the city was really still, sound of boats on the river . . . the barges . . . that old Victorian sound, it felt it could have been seventy

or eighty years ago.
And I was thinking ... listen ... I was thinking! – We
never get *close* to the past because we always *overestimate* how
different it was.
Another planet – it was not!

Daphne That's an interesting thought, Mr Lynn-Thomas
– but I must ask you to –

Robbie Why have you got drunk, Clive? Now? Tell me –

Clive Why have I got drunk? Because of you, Robbie –
you're facing a challenge, to loosen your approach for that
huge audience tomorrow, and I thought I'd get a little less
constricted myself.

Takes a long drag on cigarette.

And I want to give you one thing while I'm in this free
flowing state, and that one thing is – the Bakawanga
Paradox.

Robbie The Backerwacker *what*!

Clive The Bakawanga Paradox.

Daphne And what is that?

Clive Bakawanga being a far away place – any Far Away
place would do, any that comes into your mind ...
The Bakawanga Paradox is simply ...

He takes a drag.

'The more we hear the News from Abroad – directly from
abroad – the more insular we become.'
The more we know, the less we want to know.

Arnos *enters, giving a nod of greeting to* **Daphne***, the others
alarmed as* **Clive** *sits drunk centre stage.* **Dredge** *flicks his
cigarette out of his hand spiriting it away.*

Arnos Working late ... Admirable! No need to get up.

Clive *(hasn't moved at all)* But *despite* this paradox, Mr
Grove – I believe passionately in the mass audience, and

their ability to rise to any challenge. Their willingness to respond to different voices – different races.

Arnos   Absolutely, Clive. Absolutely.

Clive (*dangerous smile, uninhibited manner*)   But do *you* believe it? I want to know, Arnos. Do *you* really believe that.

Arnos   Sharp questioning tonight, I see! (*Beams at them.*) I just dropped by to say hello to you all ... (*He sees* **Isabel**.) And I know you too – don't I, audience sampling ... (*He greets her.*) Good evening – absolutely! ...
(*He looks at them all.*) You may wonder *why I* am here, as Head of the Spoken Word, rather than my colleague the Head of Variety. The truth is, I'm now Acting Head of all Programmes – no, no need to say anything ...
So – good luck. Don't despair at the short notice. Do your best with the lack of stars.
Never forget who's listening – the size of the audience – you'll be speaking to two continents, and some of Europe too.
After the Coronation, it's quite amazing the spread of our service. We serve the world.
The DG will be listening, and the Head of NBC ... and who knows what other high placed personages –

Clive (*suddenly*)   Don't frighten them any more, Arnos! You're scaring them – (*Putting his arm round him.*) Come on, you need a drink ...

Arnos   A most excellent plan. But outside the building, of course.

Clive   Of course ...! (*As they exit.*) You don't mind me calling you 'Arnos'...?

Daphne   That was close (*She move sharply.*) I think the best thing is for all of us to pop across the road too. *I* certainly need to. We've practised enough for today.
Come on, everyone, at the double ... time is precious.

Daphne *leads the girls off.*
Robbie *and* **Isabel** *are left.* **Mabs** *is in a corner staring at his*

leather script folder, slowly turning pages.

Robbie Clive is an amazing man, isn't he!

Isabel He certainly is . . .

Robbie He has such an effect on me, spurring me on, to take risks, to be more . . . (*He stops.*)

Isabel Subversive?

Robbie Yes . . .

He looks at **Isabel**.

And the two of you . . .

Isabel Seem so perfect for each other? We must do . . .

Robbie (*watching her*) He is lucky to have you.

Isabel Does he have me?

Silence.

Robbie (*glancing at* **Mabs** *in the corner*) Mabs? . . . Mabs?

Mabs Just got to study this, because something very complicated seems to have happened to Inspector Bonnington. Don't want to let the side down . . . It's a big thing tomorrow.

Isabel (*staring across at* **Robbie**) I was thinking about you in Blackpool.

Robbie You were . . . ? As you stood on the promenade, spying on those people.

Isabel Yes. I had the time! (*She lights a cigarette.*) Occasionally I had rather dark thoughts – but then I thought of you.

She smiles, takes a drag.

You like boys as well as girls, don't you, Robbie?

Robbie What a question . . . !

Isabel Don't worry, I'm not shockable. (*She laughs.*) How could I be after all my voyeurism! . . . (*Glancing upstage.*) And Mabs is too concerned about Inspector Bonnington.

Robbie (*looking across at her*)   How did you know to ask that? Been observing me, like all your other subjects?

Isabel   Naturally.

Robbie   Well, I'm not ashamed to admit it. Though I must be careful, especially here. I think there are many many more people like me, lots of them, that –

Isabel   Of course, that goes without saying. (*She is moving, preoccupied, smoking.*)

Robbie   Mabs?

Mabs (*still deep in study*)   I've played all these various bishops and doctors, and even dentists in the past – now I seem to have received the most enormous promotion . . . to Head of State!

Robbie (*lightly, to* **Isabel***, lowering his voice*)   I've always had . . . how to put this . . . appetites, in every direction – indulgent, sensual, I don't know what you'd call it . . . ! Food too – stuffing myself! Since I was a boy. (*Smiles.*) But I try to keep it separate, away from the workplace.

Isabel   Of course. That's very sensible. Very professional.

Robbie   As a boy I didn't just lust – I had ideas. Such ideas . . . ! (*Suddenly.*) D'you think what Clive said about the past is true? – We exaggerate how different it was . . . That must be wrong surely?! It *was* very different.

Isabel   He didn't mean *our* past . . .

Robbie   I know, but even so . . . (*He stops,* **Isabel** *moving, preoccupied.*) Isabel? What is it?

Isabel   It's not serious. (*Suddenly.*) Robbie, will you do something for me?

Robbie   What?

Isabel   It may seem odd . . . (*Indicating all the sound effect* *objects.*) I'd like you to make these work.

Robbie Those? Why, of course? What do you want?

Isabel Do me some horses ... horses' hooves ... that's nice, not too fast, clip clop, that's right ... and now some bells, country bells ... good.

Robbie Were you brought up in the country too?

Isabel Yes.

Robbie In a nice posh house?

Isabel Of course. Not too big. It was only about fifty miles from where you were working in the fields.
The War – remember – when we were children ... I was nine, and I was on my own a lot, during the War ... I had a pony. (*She smiles at the horses' hooves sound.*) I rode around, I had long blonde hair, on a white pony ... it was so quiet.

Isabel I followed the telegraph boys ... you know, bringing the telegrams, often containing the most terrible news. I'd follow them sometimes down the drives of these big houses, as they delivered their devastating messages ... I'd see the front doors open ... Nobody took much notice of a little girl on a pony, watching it all.
I heard shrieking often, the wails from inside, as the mother of the house read the news about her son.

Robbie (*quiet, touched*) I never saw anything like that.

Isabel *takes the microphone, holding it tightly.*

Isabel I rode all over ... I came upon a woman crying alone, in a field one time, curled up in a ball, such terrible sobs of grief, like her whole soul had been torn out.
It was the saddest sight I ever saw.

She holds microphone, breathes into it.

Remember the songs of that time ... ?

Robbie Of course. (*Starts to sing a few lines of a First World War song.*)

Isabel That's right.

Mabs *joins in without looking up, automatically joining in with a song he knows.* **Robbie** *and* **Mabs** *sing for a moment.*

Isabel If you could have heard those cries, Robbie – *and then broadcast them.*

She mimes a cry into microphone.

Like your idea of the children on the lake . . . there wouldn't be a war if people heard those, it certainly would have stopped that one.
That sound going into everybody's front room. It would've stopped it there and then.

Mabs (*suddenly looks up*) Where is everybody? – Good Lord, have they gone for a drink without me . . . I certainly need it as much as them.

Mabs *exits purposefully. Silence.*

Isabel (*smiles*) Robbie . . . hold me. Please.

Robbie *hesitates.*

Isabel Just come and hold me.

Robbie (*moving*) It's not right is it? (*Gently.*) We both mind about Clive.

Isabel I just want you to hold me . . . (*Looking across at him.*) Robbie . . .

Robbie *puts his arms round her.*

Isabel Hold me tight.

Robbie (*warm smile*) Anyway we're not allowed to touch here – this is the British Broadcasting Corporation.

Isabel I don't work here, remember, I don't know any of those ridiculous rules.

Robbie (*holding her tight*) Oh, Isabel, I want tomorrow to be all right . . . For that huge audience. I want it to be something special, more than just 'Friday Night at Eight'.

Isabel It will be fine. Just don't look down.
Leap – and then don't look down again . . . not even for a
second.

The music starts, the rhythmic beginning of the new introduction of
'Friday Night at Eight'. It is hushed to start with, but continues to
play until it flowers into full melody at the start of the show.
As **Isabel** *and* **Robbie** *exit, the lights change. One red light on.*
Dredge *enters in rich showgirl costume followed by* **Mabs** *in*
military uniform, white and gold braid, and medals.

Mabs Don't breathe too fast, Mabs . . .

Dredge I feel good. I feel I'm ready to take on the
world. (*She grins.*) But is the world ready for me?!

Mabs Oh, Susan – I've never been in the vanguard
before, in the vanguard of anything. I have always regarded
myself as the most old-fashioned person I know.
And now I'm on the brink of the unknown, an old dog
being blown along by a great wind.

Daphne *enters.*

Daphne Now, Mabs, remember, you must keep up with
Robbie, keep watching, keep alert, you must follow him,
wherever he goes.

Mabs I will. I will. My reactions will be lightning quick.

Robbie *enters in full dinner jacket and tails.*

Robbie Mabs will do fine. (*To* **Daphne***, quiet, close.*)
You're sure you're happy?

Daphne I'm happy – (*She smiles.*) at the moment.

Robbie I'm allowed to deviate? Now's the time to say . . .

Daphne You're allowed . . . in moderation.

Robbie (*kisses her on the cheek*) You're much bolder than
you look, Daphne . . . always have been.

Music getting more insistent. **Clive** *enters.*

Clive I have my ticket. Even though it's only senior management allowed to watch, and me – we have to have tickets.

Daphne (*suddenly*) Where on earth is Milly? Tonight of all nights! Ready, everyone ... (*She exits urgently.*)

Clive So, I'll take my seat among the exclusive gathering up there.

Robbie No, no, I can't have that. I want you here.

Clive Here, but I'll be seen!

Robbie Who'll see you!? The audience that matters can't see you.
I need you right here. Your authority, your encouragement, your inspiration.

Clive (*smiles*) Why? What can I do? For once you're out of my control.

Robbie *indicates* **Clive**'s *position upstage.*

Robbie Don't move – I'll be visiting you from time to time.

Milly *comes running on.*

Milly It was just my make-up! Had to get it right ... Robbie, I'm ready. (*She positions herself at the microphone.*) I always knew your show was the one to be on ... America! ...

The two **Dancing Girls** *come on in vivid dancing costumes as the second red light flicks on. Drum roll. The young* **Assistant**'s *voice booms out.*

Assistant 'This is the National Programme. And tonight we're joined by the NBC network in America, as we hand over to the Variety studio for ...'

Robbie *standing without script, he has cast it on the floor during this announcement. He is free.*

Robbie   Good evening, ladies and gentlemen.
And tonight we have a special programme for you . . .
(*Breaks into song.*) And first we have to warm up the band.
(*Does his hand signals.*) Hit it boys . . . hit it . . . The girls are
shimmering here – you should see what they're wearing –
they're so explosive the Archbishop of Canterbury may well
be complaining.

Hand signals to quieten the music.

We're on a journey here, hold on tight!
First a shock announcement for our English listeners, we
have killed Inspector Bonnington, he met a tragic end
falling down the stairs at his club. Welcome news, wasn't it,
Sergeant Ostler?!

Mabs (*with script, but realising* **Robbie** *is darting in and out of
it*)   It was very unexpected, certainly, sir.

Robbie   And deeply final. And crawling out of the
shadow of Bonnington is your new boss, Ostler, and he is –

Suddenly he breaks into outrageous Chico Marx Italian-style accent.

Inspector Curioso!
Yes I am Curioso. I do not put up with any fools! I'm
unafraid of anybody. *I am Curioso of the Yard*!

Mabs (*as Ostler*)   I'll have to get used to being shouted at
a lot more, sir, won't I?

Robbie (*as Curioso*)   Yes, Ostler, I am afraid I'm just that
little bit more rude than the Bonnington.
I cannot stand most members of the public . . . if people lie
to me . . . I just want to bang their heads together!
(*Dangerous.*) And I WILL do it! Most of all I hate, absolutely
loathe, your British understatement.
I am Inspector Curioso – and I will scream if I want to!

Mabs   And our first case, I believe, takes us in amongst
the aristocracy, isn't that right, sir?

Robbie (*as Curioso*)   We go to the wedding of the century,

to solve a murder among titled folk. The Farquhar-
Buzzards, the Rowlatt-Coopers, the Mallerby-Dealeys –
Curioso sniffs out the darkness that lies behind these stupid
long names!

Music changes, and the sound effects mingle, worked by **Dredge**
and the **Dancing Girls**.

And we'll also be going GLOBAL, we're going EPIC . . .

We're in an aeroplane now . . . we're skimming along Fifth
Avenue in New York.

Milly (*sings*)   America, calling calling America . . . hello
America.

Music changes.

Robbie   We're taking you with us, America.

Milly *sings*.

Robbie   You can't get off, oh no, we're climbing
upwards, we're soaring away, away from America, we can
see the great liners steaming below us on the ocean . . .

Music changes.

And now we're skimming across Europe, the palaces of
Europe!

Milly (*sings*)   The world is small . . . the world is getting
smaller.
We're just one world . . . joined by the magic of radio.

Robbie   The world is indeed small –
We're veering upwards now, climbing really high, don't fall
out, still with us, America!
And we're banking now, and we're going into our dive.
We're diving now!

And below us . . . there is Herr Hitler, and Dr Goebbels,
the master of propaganda . . . and Herr Goering . . . they
are in the Reich Palace, they have just come back from a
shooting party, and they've got rid of all their aggression
harmlessly on a lot of tiny little birds . . . ! – and now we're

flying towards them, through the great doors of the palace, past all the palace guards – they are waiting to welcome us ... waiting to welcome the flower of *British* broadcasting!

Mabs *become Hitler.*

Mabs (*as Hitler*)   Heil Hitler! Heil 'Friday Night at Eight'! We listen to you often! We're eager to hear pleasant British voices! And that particular English humour!

Robbie (*to audience*)   Milly Dews is going to sing what we think could be – we can't be sure – but what we think could be, what we hope, is Herr Hitler's favourite song ...

Milly *begins to sing softly.*

Robbie   It's not what you expect, is it? It's quite gentle, isn't it. Simple and gentle ... we won't quarrel with that.

Robbie *moves over to* **Clive** *as* **Milly** *sings softly.*

Robbie (*whispers*)   I've finished us both, do you think?

Clive (*grins*)   I don't think people will assume I was involved with that!

Robbie   But you are ... (*Softly.*) You have made me – made me different anyway. You don't think I've crossed a line. Do you – the line of what's acceptable?

Clive   Very close. Extremely close. But not *quite* over. Be careful not to use any real names though, won't you, Robbie. Those aristocrats ... don't call them by their actual names.

Robbie   Right ... (*Music playing.*) Do you approve, Clive?

Clive   Oh yes. I most certainly do. (*Smiles.*) God knows what the powers that be will make of it ... Herr Hitler shooting little birds!

Robbie   I feel the strength of the machine, like you said. I really do ... I've got America there ... right now! It's like I can see the whole mass of them there, across the ocean. And *I'm speaking to them*! It's so powerful.

Clive Told you so.

Robbie I will do your project, Clive. I will soon.
We have a pact, a pact that nobody will break. You will
see.

He moves, as **Milly** *sings softly.*

But now, watch where I go now, I *know* where to go – with
all those countries listening.

*He moves back to the microphone, he does a signal to musicians
intensifying the romantic, lyrical mood.*

Boys, come on now, expressive now, follow me, boys, that's
better. As deeply felt as you can make it.

He turns back to audience.

We're travelling, friends . . . below us through the clouds,
we're crossing boundaries, we're crossing borders, these
European countries, they're so close together . . .

We have swooped in our aeroplane . . . and seen into the
eyes of dictators, and we have no quarrel with them, and
they have no quarrel with us.

We've flown over people out working in the fields . . . and
we've flown over factories belching smoke – the workers all
look very much like those back home.

(*Sings.*) The world is small . . . and getting smaller . . .

And now where is this, where are we going now? We are
in a forest, a beautiful forest, we are skimming above the
trees.

We fly over a girl, a young girl with blonde hair, galloping
on a white pony . . .

And now we're in a glade in the forest . . . there are no
quarrels here . . . we see the very best in each other . . . the
most magical music is playing . . .
It is a golden wood and everything is peaceful here.

This is where we're landing. This is the end of our journey.

He sings softly.

This is our destination ... this is our place.

He sings softly.

This is our place.

Fade.

Act Two

Scene One

The **Assistant** *is high above the stage, reading the news in a soothing, authoritative voice. He is much more confident now.*

As the **Assistant** *reads, the lights gradually come up on the stage, early evening sunlight. Three large mailbags, bursting with letters, in the middle of the stage. Downstage* **Clive** *is sitting smoking.*

Daphne *comes on, dragging another large mailbag. She stares down at the letters, takes a deep breath, and then slips her arms deep into the letters.*

Assistant (*reading*) 'The Thames seems to have absorbed the weekend rains, its flow is much steadier, and its level is expected to fall severely in the next day or two.'

Daphne (*to herself*) I have to . . .
I have to read them all . . .

Assistant (*reading*) 'All the sides of the House of Commons found themselves in complete agreement during the debate last night on preserving the natural beauty of the countryside . . .'

Clive (*watching* **Daphne**) I like that . . . you immersing yourself in the listeners' letters.

Daphne *jumps up startled.*

Daphne I didn't see you there, I had no idea –

Clive Testing their temperature, are you?

Daphne I've been reading them all day, of course –
It's a terribly mixed reaction.

Clive At least they're responding – maybe your audience have woken at last from their deep sleep.

Daphne (*picking a letter out of the sack at random*) Mrs

Warmsley from Teddington ... (*She reads.*) 'I feel I must write to you about your new detective, your hysterical foreign policeman, Mr Curioso. I have to tell you I have never heard anything like it before ... the announcer should have prepared us for such a violent change. I had to turn down the volume more than once ...'

Clive   Yes ... they're so used to the old patterns, every show identical ... suddenly they hear a different sound.

Daphne (*moving*)   I was holding on to the rail up there so tight while it was happening, and I was shaking all over. Robbie was like he was possessed – but he never went completely through the roof, did he? ... Didn't let me down ...
Despite everything, he has a strong, practical streak in him.

Clive   He does.

Robbie *enters with* **Bernard**.
Robbie *is in everyday clothes holding a fistful of letters. He is reading a letter as he enters.*

Robbie   Mrs Percy Moorcroft, from Cirencester ... 'You should be ashamed of yourself, making fun of Scotland Yard like that, you will have harmed its worldwide reputation. What's more I've been to many weddings in the country, especially in Buckinghamshire, and none I've attended have remotely resembled the wedding portrayed in "Inspector Curioso Investigates" – It was a gross distortion.' (*He grins.*) I can't stop reading them! However bad they get ...!

Bernard   You know I was listening to it with a group of visitors from abroad ... and they all took Inspector Curioso very seriously! They analysed it, they said he screams all the time because nobody is listening to him – he is isolated from his colleagues, he is violently depressed because he is an outcast from Scotland Yard! (*He is helping himself to letters.*)

Daphne   Put those back please, they are only for the eyes of BBC personnel.

Robbie   But Bernard is the instigator of Curioso! His foreign observation – oh yes – noticed a character, a rude waiter . . . and that sparked it off in my mind.

Bernard   Yes. I come to England and what is my contribution to the culture – I help create a detective, isn't that amazing! (*He laughs.*) In the land of Conan Doyle and Miss Agatha Christie – I invent a sleuth.

Clive   The interesting thing is –

Robbie (*sharp grin*)   Tell us what the interesting thing is.

Clive (*lightly*)   The fascinating thing is – the portrayal of Hitler, your flight of peace over Europe . . . all of it has gone completely unnoticed! The only thing that has struck them is Curioso – even if they hate it.

Daphne   Yes – it's too early to say if we should ever do it again after today.

Robbie   Oh we've got to keep going for two more shows at least – what harm can it do – then we'll bring back Bonnington I promise!

Daphne (*briskly*)   Well, we'll have to see how this week goes –

Robbie   There's been no reaction at all from America, Clive . . . I must have fallen like a stone . . .

Daphne   Right, there's work to be done! (*Indicating* **Bernard**.) And your friend shouldn't be here now, Robbie . . . (*To* **Clive**.) And I can't believe you're smoking again . . . (*She moves.*) It's time to prepare for the next broadcast.

Robbie   Yes, yes. (*Suddenly.*) Listen to this, Daphne! (*To* **Clive**.) This will drive her wild, watch this . . . !

Robbie *does his hand signals, the musicians start to play, a strong insinuating melody.*

Daphne   This is childish . . . !

Robbie (*grinning broadly*)   Play it louder, boys . . . give it everything!

Daphne   This is a very obvious way to try to provoke me.

Clive   It's not obvious to the rest of us – why is this music so powerful, Robbie?

Robbie   Because it is my *own* composition. It's against all the rules to play your own composition on your own broadcast. Crazy, isn't it!

Daphne   It will never happen while I'm around . . . I can assure you. (*She exits.*)

Bernard   I must rush too, to get back in time to listen. One day maybe I will be allowed to watch from here. You should have a live audience . . . fill it with all sorts of normal people, off the streets, it'd be exciting!

Robbie   'Normal people'! (*He smiles.*) You mean like Baron Freiher von Brandis?

Bernard *smiles and exits.* **Robbie** *alone with* **Clive**. *The musicians are still playing* **Robbie***'s composition softly.*

Robbie   I haven't forgotten – our project.

Clive   I should hope not . . .

Robbie   We must prepare ourselves to strike, to do the presentation –

Clive   Yes. I have a plan.

Robbie (*smiles*)   Of course you do.

Clive   To get round their objections about balance – it is always the problem – the dreaded *balance* . . . I'm going to propose that our German programme is *one of a series* of documentaries – so we'll do the Irish potato famine . . . one about slavery in the Deep South of the United States . . . and one about a mining disaster here, and its effect on a pit village . . .
We do Germany first, of course.
If it's one of several planned programmes, they will not object.

Robbie Terrific. They won't be expecting that . . . But you will wait for me to present it to them – won't you?

Clive Of course.

Robbie You're tremendous at planning, but I'm good at the showbiz flattery . . . Just need a little of that with Arnos. We are a team, the bumpkin and the cat.

Clive What does that mean . . . sounds like a nursery rhyme?

Robbie No. I like it. The bumpkin and the cat. I'm the rustic, with bits of soil still dropping off me on to the microphone – and you're the urban cat . . . – slinking around, poised, planning silently, stalking its quarry! Together we can be such a powerful combination.

Clive Yes, that's the idea.

Robbie (*as they both move to exit*) And do you like the tune? I think it might be a real winner, don't you? (*He grins.*) Maybe I can get Milly to sing it on her trip to Vienna?!

Blackout. **Robbie**'s *tune continues to play before cutting out.*

Scene Two

Broadcasting House.

Isabel *sitting on bench as if waiting outside an office. She has a large pile of papers and folders.* **Clive** *upstage reading a novel.*

Isabel You want to go through anything one last time?

Clive No, I'm pretty clear – there's no need for any late adjustments.

The **Assistant** *appears. His manner is now confident and corporate.*

Assistant Mr Grove is overrunning, just a fraction, because of a rather important guest. (*He looks around.*) But you're not even all here!

Isabel   Mr Penacourt *is* here.

Clive   He's just wandered off because of the wait. (*He turns a page of his book.*) It's taken a long time to get us all together – and much as I love rereading Flaubert, we're not going to miss our appointment, I assure you.

Assistant   No, well, it's a big day all round, isn't it, I mean with Mr Penacourt having his first *really live* audience, in the studio. Have you seen the guest list, it makes remarkable reading, I assure you – quite unprecedented.

Robbie (*as he enters*)   I'm glad you think so.

Robbie *is expensively dressed, wearing a buttonhole. The patina of success all over him.*

Assistant   So you are here.

Robbie   Of course.

Assistant (*his manner to* **Robbie** *sycophantic*)   I'm sure Mr Grove won't be long now.

Robbie   I hope there's a good reason why we're being kept waiting.

Assistant   Oh *there is*. I promise you. (*He smiles.*) There definitely is! (*He exits.*)

Clive (*turns page of book nonchalantly*)   Sounds intriguing . . .

Robbie   It better be. There's something about that bloke – you trained him too well, Clive.

Clive   He's inoffensive, still finding his way . . .

Isabel (*to* **Robbie**)   Treated you with a lot of respect, didn't he. (*Teasing smile.*) Somebody from Variety being talked to like that!

Robbie (*grins*)   Of course. Well he could hardly do anything else after what's happened these last weeks.

Isabel (*mock innocent*)   Oh, what is that?

Robbie *turns slowly, shocked.*

Isabel Your face. His face!

Robbie For a moment I believed you. Believed you knew nothing.

He sits next to her.

(*Softly.*) Will I ever see you alone again?

Isabel (*smiles*) And why should you want to do that?

Robbie (*warmly, but not too intimate*) Because you always surprise me . . .

Clive *turns page of book upstage.*

Isabel (*to* **Robbie**) I know exactly what you're after.

Robbie (*innocently*) And what is that?

Isabel When I'm 'observing' in my bus queues and those cheap cafés, have I heard people talking about *you*, about Curioso . . . ??
(*She smiles.*) Go on, tell me that's not what you're thinking, look me in the eyes and deny it.

Robbie (*staring at her*) I was not thinking *that*.

Isabel (*lightly*) Nobody has ever told a bigger lie!

Clive (*calling from upstage*) Even I have heard things – while walking across Waterloo Bridge.

Robbie Even you, Clive!

Isabel It's amazing – Curioso's catchphrases like 'I'm Curioso and I will scream if I want to' . . . I've heard building workers shout it to each other as they hang on to the scaffolding . . . I've heard children yelling it in back gardens . . . people can't get it out of their heads.
It's like for the first two or three weeks, it was a bit of a surprise, and then they moved into a whole other gear and became obsessed by Curioso.
(*Warm smile.*) It's spread like flu.

Robbie (*to* **Isabel**) And for the first time people know who I am, when I say my name. They still don't recognise me. (**Isabel** *makes a sorrowful noise*, **Robbie** *grins*.) But that may change, I'm doing some articles and photo spreads this week.

Clive (*calmly*)   And then you will become a full London celebrity.

Robbie   If only I could *change* my name. This idiotic name I chose, Penacourt, it's too late now! When I first became an actor – I saw it on a mansion block in St John's Wood.

Turns unabashed to **Isabel**.

Tell me more of what people are saying, what you hear.

Isabel (*laughing*)   I can't believe this – not only am I useful to Clive, now I'm useful to you too! Reporting to you on your audience . . .
But actually I'm going to disappoint you. I have just moved on. I'm at the Ministry of Information now, part of a government department.

Clive   She's always been able to get any job she's applied for.

Isabel (*her mood vivacious*)   I'm now in charge of bringing all these reports together, collating the mass observation research . . . and I'm surrounded by all these awful twits who make a point of pretending they don't know anything about the modern world. (*She mimics*.) 'Oh I never listen to the wireless, I only go to the opera . . . !' The very place where all this information about the general public is ending up – is the only place they haven't heard of *you*!

Robbie (*warm smile*)   So you're going to *blend* in there as well – become a very British civil servant.

Isabel   Well, they think I'm rather exotic at the moment, (*Smiles*.) because I'm clearly female, and also I have loitered around, as they call it, in all sorts of dodgy areas of this town.

Dredge *enters*.

Robbie   Dredge!

Dredge (*approaching*)   Never been allowed on this floor before! Been moving really slowly to make the most of it . . .

Robbie (*looking at her figure*)   I'm sure they've been appreciating that up here.

Dredge   Daphne wants to know – 'You will be along shortly, won't you, because there's some complicated final rehearsals' . . . that's how she put it.

Robbie   Tell her I will be. Just got to do this.

Dredge   I'll tell her we should start without you. (*She grins.*) That's what it sounds like to me!

Dredge *moves to exit.*

Robbie   It's marvellous to see her really confident – with the success of the show, she's really glowing. (*Calling after her.*) And, Dredge – I'm not going to call you that any more! Susan, it'll be Susan.

Dredge *turns.*

Dredge   About time, Robbie! (*She exits.*)

Robbie   I don't know how I could have called her that for so long.

Arnos *enters. He is accompanied by a tall man with a short moustache.*

Arnos   Oh, there you are – we've been in conference.

Robbie   Yes – well, we've been out here for quite a while . . .

Arnos (*to his companion*)   This is Mr Penacourt here . . . (*He turns.*) and this is Mr Walt Disney.

Robbie (*startled*)   Mr Disney . . .

Walt   Oh, this is Mr Penacourt? – how interesting to meet you.

Robbie (*stunned*)   You've heard of me?!

Walt   But of course I have. One of the reasons I'm here in this building.

Arnos   Mr Disney has come for a guided tour of Broadcasting House.

Robbie (*suddenly worried*)   It's not because I did some of the voices of the dwarfs from *Snow White* on my show – you're not concerned about that? That's not the reason you've heard of me?

Walt   No, no, that's not a problem.
I'm interested in some of your creations, that you've done on the radio here. I think they're quite wide creations, that Curioso fellow for instance.

Arnos   Mr Disney has been able to appreciate some of your broadcasts.

Robbie   That's wonderful. (*Nervous, respectful.*) What d'you mean exactly by wide creations?

Walt   They could be appreciated all over the world, yes, across national barriers . . .

Clive   Well, certainly you know all about that, Mr Disney – *Snow White* has caused something of a sensation, hasn't it, all over the place.

Walt   A sensation? That's a big word, and big words can make me nervous . . .

Isabel   I loved it. I've seen it three times so far.

Walt (*genial*)   Well, your Royal Family gave me lunch – so we must be doing something right.
And in Germany too, it's gone down a storm . . . (*He chuckles.*) I doubt the service will be as good though.
I've been saying to Mr Grove, anyhow, we've been agreeing . . . vitality without crudity – that is the universal language.

Arnos   Of course, one can have too much vitality.

Walt   You most certainly can! Some of my artists keep
trying to do things with Mickey Mouse as jokes amongst
themselves, they do things with that mouse that are so
obscene – (*To* **Isabel**.) excuse me – I doubt you'd find
them in the animal kingdom.
I fire them at once, of course.

Clive (*sharp grin*)   And there are no union problems, are
there?!

Walt   Oh no, we don't have unions, we don't need unions
. . . Some things can't be avoided though – I have a few
Jews, working for me, (*Genial.*) one rather has to where I
come from – need to use the talent . . .

Clive looks at **Arnos**. **Walt** *moves.*

Walt   So, Mr Penacourt, I must get on.
But I would very much like to have a meeting with you
before I leave the country, very interested in taking this
further.

He looks around.

Who owns the copyright of this little fellow Curioso?

Arnos   That can all be worked out –

Walt (*to* **Robbie**)   Yes I'm sure we can do business. I
happen to know some Live Action Hollywood producers
are on your tail too. It's all go!

Silence. They look at **Robbie** *for his response.*

Robbie   Forgive me, I'm so surprised.
I had no idea anybody had heard of me in America.

Walt   Oh yes, the word is out. (*Genial smile.*) And the word
is good.
And the reason is – you understand what is important. If
you speak to the child in people – you speak to the world.

He begins to move off with **Arnos**.

We grapple, don't we, with the power we've been given –
grapple to use it well.

(*As he exits.*) I know somebody else will tell you this, so don't take offence if I mention it, but you must think of changing your name.

Walt *exits*.

Arnos (*in exit*) I will just see Mr Disney to his next port of call. (*He follows* **Walt**.)

Isabel So Mr Disney seems to like you, Robbie!

Robbie *full of thoughts, churning with excitement.*

Robbie Yes . . . yes.

Clive Just shows you, do something on the wireless and *absolutely* everybody is listening . . .

Robbie It's amazing, isn't it. All that interest from America! My heart's pumping, my head's about to burst! (*He is pacing.*) I should tell Daphne . . . I must tell Daphne! (*He stares upstage.*)

Clive (*calmly*) You're not in the mood to face Arnos, are you?

Robbie I will be . . . I said I would.

He turns.

Maybe not. (*He looks at both of them.*) No . . .

Clive (*breezily*) Don't worry, I can do it on my own.

Isabel And I'll be there, Robbie, (*Tapping her file.*) with all my facts.

Robbie It's just, yes . . . I need to take everything in . . . everything that's happened.

Clive Of course.

Robbie (*turns in exit*) Just do the first part, Clive, don't do the full negotiation.

Clive Why not?

Robbie You *can* be a little abrupt you know –

Clive You're giving *me* lessons now. . . ! Go on – your
dancing girls are waiting.

Arnos *enters*.

Arnos I have deposited Mr Disney with NRD.
I'm ready for you now.

Blackout.

Scene Three

Music playing softly, it is **Robbie** *singing. A recording.*
Arnos *is sitting behind a desk.* **Clive** *and* **Isabel** *facing him,*
standing.

Arnos You don't mind me listening to Mr Penacourt
singing . . . it's a medley from last week's show.

He stares at both of them for a moment

Interesting meeting Mr Disney, wasn't it?

Clive (*smiles*) It could hardly fail to be . . .

Arnos Don't worry I'm not dazzled by it – I can assure
you. The fact that we have an American mogul, an
entrepreneur touring the building is exciting a lot of people.
NRD was bowing and scraping just now. But I'm not
dazzled.
So Clive – you want to do something about what's
happening in Germany . . . ?

Clive (*surprised he knows*) Yes –

Arnos To be more precise – you want to draw attention
to the restrictions that are being applied to the Jews?

Clive Yes . . . and –

Arnos And you somehow want to use Mr Penacourt in
all of this?

Clive You're very well-informed. I'd be interested to
know how you came by all this information.

Arnos   I'm the Head of Programmes – it's my business to know what's going on.

Arnos *suddenly seems more formidable. His blubbery bland face stares back at them.*

Isabel (*to* **Clive**)   Shall we move on . . . to the substance of the proposal?

Arnos (*to* **Clive**)   You should, yes. You know, Miss Ellison – we're finding your sampling, that audience response business, most intriguing, by the way . . .

Isabel   Yes, well, that's one of the reasons I'm here – in case that comes up, you have to know how to read those findings, you can't just take them at face value.

Arnos   Quite – a useful reminder . . .

Robbie *singing softly in the background.*

Arnos   I like this song. Do you like this number? It's an old tune of course – but with a new twist.

Clive   I have a plan, Mr Grove, an important plan, so the programme which I'm about to describe cannot be thought in any way to be a provocation. Our German neighbours will *not* be able to think that.
The question of balance . . . it can be solved . . . if we do a *series* of documentaries, one about the Irish potato famine, which clearly involves *us* . . . *our* responsibility.

Arnos (*casually*)   We have just commissioned a Talk about the Irish famine.

Clive (*startled*)   You have?! Well, a series can be made out of other . . .

Arnos   We have also commissioned a Talk on slavery in the Deep South, and a documentary on a mining disaster and its effect on a pit village . . .

Clive *is stunned . . . his normal effortless composure is being strained.*

Clive   Who's been talking to you?

Arnos (*bland smile*)   I talk to everyone.
These are ideas that arose through the normal processes.

Clive   So – my German programme can fit amongst
these –

Arnos *looks at* **Clive**.

Arnos   No – we don't know when we will be broadcasting
them. You can't smuggle the programme in that way, I'm
afraid. Argue your case for it, on its own.

Isabel (*worried at* **Clive**'*s tightening mood*)   Yes, Clive . . .
you should do that.

Clive *paces for a second.*

Clive   I put it to you, the British are a fair-minded
people, some of the most fair-minded people in the world,
and they deserve to be told the truth, about what's
happening . . .

Arnos   Truth is always difficult, isn't it.
Truth can be a very different thing to different people.

Clive   Facts then, facts are not difficult.
I want to make the audience live a day through the eyes of
a Jewish man and his family, in *Germany now.* Show him
trying to go about his business . . . and the new rules he
has to obey.

Arnos   It is not our job to overdramatise current events.

Clive (*very sharp*)   I'm not talking about overdramatising,
I'm talking about reporting what's happening and making it
vivid.

Arnos   And the evidence varies – about how harsh things
are, and they may be temporary.
By the time you've finished your programme – and you're
not quick, Clive – all these restrictions may have changed.

Clive (*sharp*)   I doubt that will happen.

Arnos   We have to of course be very careful about
anti-Semitism in *this* country. It is undeniable there is

anti-Semitism, in the mass of the population ... that is a
regrettable fact of life.
If there *was* to be a war ... people wouldn't necessarily
respond to the idea of fighting for some foreign Jews –
We've been looking at some information on the subject –

Isabel   This is where I come in, Mr Grove ... because
there has been some research, you're right, and I took part
in it. And the 'research' amounts to little anecdotes about
chance anti-Semitic remarks people had made at bus
queues and in other public places, we're processing it now
at the Ministry of Information – and it's a totally random
selection ... and the degree of prejudice reported is quite
mild in fact. It really is.

Clive (*to* **Arnos**)   It doesn't mean people won't empathise
with real suffering when they're shown it is going on – that
is a ridiculous idea, that people will not identify with it just
because it is happening to some foreigners –

Arnos   Identify – that is a good word.

Pause. **Robbie** *singing and then an orchestral interlude playing softly
behind* **Arnos**.

Of course we always have to be very careful, because of
the appalling exaggerated stories that were reported during
the war, the Hun bayoneting babies, torture in Flanders, all
of it was bunkum of course, and the people now know it
was bunkum ...
We've got to avoid repeating that mistake of the past –
being guilty of sensationalism.

Clive   But those were ignorant rumours ... we're talking
about *facts here*. And what's more we're not an arm of the
government.

Arnos   Good Lord no! We're independent of the
government ... of course.

Clive   It's not our job to conduct the government's foreign
policy, it's our job to inform.

Arnos   Inform, absolutely.

But of course *if* there is a conspiracy of silence, which you seem to be suggesting, if there is, it is that we somehow are prepared for war, that is what the mass of people think . . . when you and I know that the preparations are pathetic! . . .

We have to watch out for that . . . we don't want to set off the avalanche . . . from Germany . . . when we're so unprepared . . .

That is why of course Mr Churchill is not invited to broadcast . . .

Clive   This is a way of educating the world . . . getting world opinion mobilised – so war is *less* likely.

Germany *does* care about world opinion. If the whole of the Empire and America were enraged about what is going on inside Germany, and above all the Catholic Church was forced to take a stand, it would be very difficult for any country to withstand that, to completely ignore it.

Arnos   Steady on, steady on . . . (*Holding up his hand.*) Now *you* are talking about influencing government policy.

Clive   I'm talking about the power of broadcasting – to convey the reality of what's happening to people.

Music playing behind **Arnos**.

Arnos   Above all we have to consider what the mass of the population will stand – and the fact is the Jewish people are prone to exaggerate – I know this from my own experience . . .

Clive   I can't believe you think this is all wild exaggeration.

Arnos   *Hard evidence.* Do you have it?

Clive   Yes.

Arnos   About people being arrested, pulled away in the middle of the night to these camps and all that . . . ? Do you have recordings of people telling us about things they have *directly* witnessed, and then their stories checked and double-checked, and confirmed by three independent

sources?
(*Very sharp.*) Do you have that?

He stares at **Clive**.

Do you have that, yes or no?

Clive   Checked by three independent sources – no.

Arnos (*sharp*)   Or even *two* independent sources?

Pause. He leans back.

And of course I'm concerned – I have to be concerned –
about the question of balance . . . if you do it in isolation,
it will seem like an act of provocation, to the Germans.

Clive (*furious but steely*)   Pleased with yourself are you . . .
your little ruse! Back where we came in – how clever.
I can't believe you're being this smug, I really *cannot* –

Isabel (*quickly*)   Shhhh . . . Clive . . . not this way . . .

Arnos   Now, now, no name-calling. I know you were
particularly close to Sir John, sadly just departed from this
organisation, but *no* name-calling. I won't stand for that.

Isabel   Clive, just take a moment . . . before you go on –

But **Clive** *is back in control.*

Clive   If I am angry, it is because this is a terribly
important topic . . . think of it as a story, as a hugely
urgent story that has to be told.

Arnos   I will absolutely consider what you've said.

Clive   You will have to do more than consider.

Arnos   I will review everything. As you've said – reporting
the facts is important.
And for your part, in return for my review – your friend,
Mr Penacourt . . . it's best not to involve him, isn't it . . .
He is making his way as one of our first true wireless stars,
created purely by the wireless. A real home-grown
achievement.
It's not appropriate, with such an important topic, to

involve an entertainer, it's not seemly, a song and dance
man, is it?
I think you will agree. Leave him alone – and I will
consider.

Blackout.

Scene Four

Broadcasting House.

Honker *and* **Walt** *standing together.* **Honker** *staring around
him, he is holding a ticket. Sound of an audience from the distance,
distant musicians warming up.*

Honker It's marvellous to be here, isn't it! Have you
been here before?

Walt No, no. I'm just waiting to be shown my seat. I'm
staying to see this Curioso character . . .

Honker Yes. Yes. He's very effective, isn't he!
He is now completely out of my range of course, Mr
Penacourt. I'll never get him back to my funny outfit now.

He turns to **Walt**.

I'm Harry 'Honker' Wallace . . . from the television side.

Walt Pleased to meet you.

Walt *doesn't introduce himself.*

Honker The formality of this place – it really hits you,
doesn't it! Even the doormen, are so terribly snooty . . .
All the power and prestige is on show, as soon as you get
through the door.

Walt Yes, they certainly make sure you feel it.

Honker (*whistles*) And of course what an audience they've
got here today . . . Unbelievable! It's a real contrast to my
garden shed approach.

Turns to **Walt**.

Are you anything to do with the business?

Walt   In a way . . .

Honker   Shouldn't think you've heard much about
television, have you? That strange flickering box we've been
playing around with over here . . . ?

Walt   I have indeed, Mr Wallace – and I can tell you I'm
very interested in it.

Honker   You are!? I'm amazed – you're one of the very
few.

Walt   I hope you grow, Mr Wallace – and grow big.

Honker (*grins*)   I don't think there's much chance of *me*
growing.

Walt (*quietly predatory*)   Just think of folks in their homes –
picture them, they've only got one outlet in their homes for
entertainment . . . the *radio*.
That's why everybody here is so grand and self-important –
at the moment they rule the roost. It's the same in my
country. They're the only ones allowed into people's homes.
No wonder *anything* on the radio, folks just drink in.

But if you can dilute that monopoly, Mr Wallace, a new
outlet, a rival in that front room, of the homes of America
– that will be very good news for people like me. (*He stares
around him.*) Very good commercial news.

Honker (*intrigued*)   People like you?

Walt   Yes, I'm in the animation business myself. But all
forms of Entertainment interest me. Today Mr Curioso
interests me . . . I see great possibilities in that little fellow.

Bernard *enters.*

Bernard   Oh, Mr Wallace – you've got a ticket too.

Walt   We've all got tickets.

Bernard (*to* **Walt**, *very formal*)   The Baron Freiher von
Brandis (*To* **Honker**.) There is such an audience for

Robbie! And people waiting in the streets, to see if they can spot him coming in and out.

Walt (*immediately interested*) People in the streets eh? . . . Good.

Assistant *comes running in.*

Assistant There you are, Mr Disney, sorry you've been kept waiting, I've come to escort you to the VIP room, which is rather embarrassingly full at the moment – we may have to open another.

Honker *looks stunned at the mention of* **Walt**'s *name.*

Walt Good luck, Mr Wallace – you grow as quick as you can.

Honker I didn't realise, I . . . I'm terribly sorry, I . . .

Assistant (*as he escorts* **Walt** *out*) This is my last day reading the news actually – I'm moving on to more important things, it's not really a job for a young man, don't you agree? (*They exit.*)

Honker Oh dear, have I made a total fool of myself . . . my chance to talk to Walt Disney . . . !

Robbie *and* **Daphne** *enter.* **Robbie** *is in his shirt sleeves. Sound of the audience getting louder.*

Honker You've just missed Mr Disney, but he's going to watch!

Daphne It's extremely exciting, isn't it. . . ! And a little nerve-racking being in the spotlight like this – but we will survive it.

Robbie We will do better than survive it. It's my last show before my summer break – so it's got to be doubly special.

Bernard It's so funny, the types of people that are here. *I* say why don't you have a live audience, and Robbie says *yes* – and who do they go and invite?! – An audience of bishops and generals!

Daphne   And the Head of the All English Lawn Tennis
Club.

Bernard   Everybody who is anybody is here – all under
one roof.

Robbie   I *have* managed to get six taxi drivers invited,
they'll be sprinkled in amongst them!

Clive *enters, his manner quiet, serious.*

Robbie (*casually*)   Clive, how are you? . . . How are
things?

Clive   I need to talk to Robbie alone . . .

Daphne   Yes – well, only a moment. (*To* **Robbie**.) Don't
let him spoil your preparations, I'm coming back in a
second, I warn you . . . (*To* **Honker** *and* **Bernard**.) Come
on, everyone . . .

Bernard   We need ringside seats! – (*As he leaves.*) We may
be sitting next to the King's doctor.

Robbie (*smiles*)   And so you should, you are a Baron, after
all!!

Robbie *and* **Clive** *alone. The sound of the musicians warming up.*

Robbie   What's happened? You didn't do the whole
presentation, did you? I *told* you to wait for me.

Clive   Somebody had briefed him.

Robbie   What do you mean?

Clive   He knew exactly what I was going to say before I
even started –

Robbie   Really? How could he have done . . . ?

Clive   Somebody had given him all the details, that's
how . . .

Robbie   Who could have done that?

Clive   I don't know. (*Slight pause.*) You haven't been
sounding off, have you, to people around this building?

Robbie   No I haven't. You think it was *ME*? I'm not that stupid, I've spoken to no one (*With force.*) Absolutely no one. It was not *me*, Clive ... (*He moves.*) You should talk to that sinister ex-assistant of yours ... !

Clive *moves.*

Clive   I was also warned off having any further involvement with you. They are obviously worried about your popularity giving our project added force.

Robbie   They tried *that*, did they ... ? I don't like the sound of that at all! They have no right ... how dare they! *I* will choose, who I consort with, who I work with ...

Clive   You've got to do it *now*, Robbie, you realise.

Robbie   Do what?

Clive   Our project. You've got to do something in this broadcast ...

Robbie   Now? *This* broadcast! Are you out of your mind?! I can't do it now.
I am completely unprepared.

Clive   Yes you can – with your powers for improvisation.

Robbie   That would be a crazy thing for me to attempt. If I start blurting out political messages, in the middle of my show – Doubly idiotic with this audience of bishops and all the other senior figures – Mr Disney too!

Clive (*forcefully*)   Robbie, you have to think of all the audience outside, forget these ridiculous VIPs.

Robbie   I'm *not* going to forget them ... this is my show ... I am a star now.
You have to realise that.

Clive   Precisely. So you won't take the risk?

Robbie   I'm not afraid of risks – I've never been afraid of risks.

Assistant   'This is the National Programme copyright

reserved. Here's the news and sports bulletins. They will be
followed by an edition of 'Friday Night at Eight', presented
tonight in front of a specially invited audience who have
come to watch in the studio.'

(*Reading news.*)   'The Foreign Secretary said in the
Commons today that the Government will bear in mind
the suggestion made by Mr Noel Baker for the despatch of
an impartial International Commission to watch events on
the frontiers between Germany and Czechoslovakia.

Robbie *moves.*

Robbie   *But* I'm not going to let them get off scot-free.
They had no right to intervene like that – to warn you off.
I will do something . . .

Clive   You must do something.

Robbie   Leave me now . . . I need a moment. I have to
work things out.

The **Assistant** *reading the news high above them.*

Clive *exits. The intro music for the show begins, rhythmic, catchy, it*
gradually gets louder and more pulsating.
Mabs, **Dredge** *and the* **Dancing Girls** *in their full dance*
costumes, and **Milly Dews** *come on. One of the* **Dancing**
Girls *gives* **Robbie** *a red jacket instead of his usual dinner jacket.*

Robbie (*quiet, to himself*)   This isn't easy . . .
(*To* **Mabs** *as the music builds.*) This may be a slightly rough
ride, Mabs.

Mabs   A rough ride? Surely not. With everything going so
well! – That's the last thing we need . . .
All my life I have never been connected with anything
that's flourished – and now here I am, in the most
amazingly flourishing set-up.
We mustn't do anything to spoil that . . . that would be
heartbreaking.

Milly (*to* **Robbie**)   I hope I hit all my high notes . . . I
can't believe the audience we are facing, people from

America, the Bishop of London.
It's such a tribute to you, of course.
Please be careful not to get up to too many of your tricks
though, Robbie ... we want something smooth and
delightful ... a bouquet of tunefulness ... that's the phrase
I've been using to myself – I have never been so nervous.

The red lights flick on.
Robbie *surveys his audience, as the music rises to a crescendo and
then it settles into a soft rhythm behind* **Robbie***'s dialogue.*

Robbie   It's Friday – and therefore it must be 'Friday
Night at Eight'.

Milly *bursts into the 'Friday Night' trill.*

Robbie   Welcome, everybody, and 'everybody' means
something different tonight.
For those of you at home, and that's all of you, of course
... let me say it should be Lords, Ladies and Gentlemen
... and the show should be called 'All under one Roof'.
(*He sings softly.*) 'All under one Roof'. Because we're
surrounded by all sorts of unexpected visitors. If I look
around you won't believe what I see – ermine-capped
slippers are tapping to the music. I can see them twitching
as I speak.

He grins.

Milly Dews is with me ... who do you see that particularly
strikes you, Milly?

Milly (*taken aback*)   Who do I see ... ?

Robbie   Yes!

Milly (*struggling*)   The ... the ... Bishop ... of
London ...

Robbie   Yes the Bishop of London is here ... ! And the
Head of the King's Needlework, The Commissioner of the
Metropolitan Police, the Royal chauffeur is here ... and
the Norwegian Ambassador!
They're all together with us!

(*He sings*.) 'We're all under one roof tonight . . .'
(*Indicates* **Dredge** *and the* **Dancing Girls**.) And the girls
look so special – so spectacular . . . they are any man's
dream.
They're too good not to be seen.
(*Staring upstage to the girls*.) So let's *see* them . . .
Come here, Susan Dredge. Approach the microphone.
Susan . . . say hello to the listening people.

Dredge *approaches nervously.*

Robbie   From the sound of her hello . . . you can conjure
her picture.

Dredge (*breathy, into microphone*)   Hello . . . hello everyone.

Robbie *plants a loud kiss on her cheek. And then sounds another
kiss into the microphone.*

Robbie   The sound of a *kiss* should help you even more
. . . all those with a romantic imagination, let it float, be
vivid.
(*He does a hand signal, music changes*.) The sound of kisses is
one of the sounds that will be heard in the special
investigation – a very particular episode – of Inspector
Curioso.

Indicates to **Milly** *who is looking distinctly uncomfortable.* **Mabs**
too is very unsure what's going to happen.

Milly (*singing the Curioso theme*)   'Inspector Curioso . . . our
new detective . . . Curioso, Curioso . . . the rudest man we
know . . . !'

Robbie   An episode of Curioso that will surprise everyone
that hears it.
We follow Curioso's first visit to London – when he arrives
in the Capital. It's not unlike somebody else's first
impression of London – your host for the evening – yes,
the voice of Curioso, Robbie Penacourt!
(*As Curioso, broad Italian*.) I come to London and I'm
surprised so much by what I see!
I see scarlet clad bishops scuttling off to secret rendezvous

... who are they going to meet?
What mysterious assignations are they keeping? – That's
what Curioso asks!
I come upon a Masonic lodge full of politicians and
members of my own Scotland Yard dressed up in ridiculous
clothes! ... I follow them down dark alleyways, to their
temples in secret cellars under Piccadilly Circus ... !
(*Suddenly to* **Mabs**.) Sergeant Ostler, we stumble, don't we,
on a conspiracy that reaches high and low!?

Mabs (*reluctantly*)   High and low, sir? ... If you say so, sir.
Certainly low, sir, does it go *high*? ... Not sure how high it
goes ...

Robbie   It goes very high. Oh yes, Ostler, very high
indeed! We find members of parliament taking money from
a foreign power, the imbeciles!

He does hand signals, intimate music.

Most of all we find the most wonderful love affairs, secret
lovers, forbidden loves – among all sorts of people. Love
stories that have never been told before.
Curioso finds the hypocrites, who say one thing in public
and love something else totally different in private. Oh yes!
The sound of the kisses ... Curioso is on their tail!

He suddenly remembers **Walt** *is watching.*

He turns to the musicians, does hand signals.

Dark, boys ... come on, dark, boys ... you can get darker
than that ... really deep down.

Back to audience.

And most interesting of all we find *betrayal* yes, oh yes, by
people so close to Curioso ... people right next to him in
Scotland Yard – they have been working against our friend
Curioso – he may have to leave these shores ... oh yes, he
very well might!

As himself.

And so ... to take us into this dark exotic mystery, yes

some music written by yours truly, Robbie Penacourt! *I*
wrote this tune!
It's called 'The strongest love I know' . . . come on, boys,
don't fiddle around, you can find the music, you can do it
– that's right . . . there she is! . . . That's the tune . . . come
on, boys, give it your all – let the folks at home hear it!

He sings a sharp, staccato lyric to his own song – relishing defying
the rules.
The red lights flick off.
Robbie'*s tune continues to play, as the lights change.* **Mabs**,
Dredge *and the* **Dancing Girls** *and* **Milly Dews** *exit.*
Robbie *takes his jacket off, lets it fall, starts taking his shoes off.*
Daphne *runs on.*

Daphne   How *dare* you – how dare you have done that!

Robbie   What have I dared to do?

Daphne   Don't try that with me, Robbie.
You know perfectly well it was a disgrace – that was inept
beyond belief.
You play your own tune on your own show against all the
rules, you wear that ridiculous jacket . . . and you do a
medley full of sexual references . . .
It was a total shambles.

Robbie *is icy-calm.*

Robbie   It seems to have held the attention of the
bishops, doesn't it?!

Dredge *enters.*

Daphne (*loud*)   And you, Susan – that was completely
uncalled for, you going to the microphone like that, it was
unprecedented.

Dredge   I didn't know what to do – he called out 'come
here, Susan' – what was I to do?!
He said to me, come and speak to the audience . . .

Robbie   I *asked* her to, remember!

Daphne (*back to* **Robbie**)   I have to tell you I have called

Mr Grove down now, so we can have a post-mortem to work out what happened – we'll see what *he* says! Because you were completely out of control, Robbie.

Robbie   Out of *control* . . . Yes I've been thinking about that during the show, Daphne . . . control. (*Goes up to her, takes her arm.*) Because somebody around here has been passing on everything to the high-ups, to the management, about my most confidential discussions with Clive.

Daphne   We're not talking about that.

Robbie   *I'm* talking about that.

Daphne   Susan, will you leave us please.

Robbie   Susan, you can stay. Let this be part of your education. (*Dangerous grin.*) 'The meaning of loyalty' – she is your boss as well after all!

Daphne   They are two totally different issues – what happened in this broadcast – and the breaking of confidences. Both will be looked into.

Robbie   You don't need to 'look into it' – you forget I'm a detective – I always solve every case. (*Getting physically close to her.*) Admit it, Daphne – go on admit it to me . . .

Daphne (*with force*)   If you're referring to the fact that I couldn't leave you completely unsupervised – *of course* I admit that.
That you couldn't be allowed to walk straight up to the microphone and address the world – without somebody senior in this building having a pretty good idea of what was going to come out. Of course I passed on everything I knew to the management – that was my job.
(*She looks at him.*) And I'm still doing it.

Robbie *is holding her close, powerfully, as if he might hurt her.*

Robbie   What about all our pledges – our promises – that we'd never do anything without each other's knowledge?

Daphne (*very forceful*)   Susan, leave us *right now* . . . Go on!

Dredge *exits.* **Daphne** *turns back to* **Robbie**.

Daphne   I'm amazed that you thought anything different would happen. But it suits you as a performer to think you are a free spirit, making up the rules as you go . . . so *I let you believe it.* Because that way you're effective.
In reality of course, everything is checked and double-checked, we keep as close a watch as we can, especially important at the present moment – so if you are spontaneous, we're pretty certain of the boundaries you're operating within. (*Their faces close.*) And I can reassure management that nothing unsafe is going to occur.

Robbie   And all those ledgers, those beautifully detailed notes you made, those were merely to keep senior management informed?

Daphne   Not all of them. Some were for us.

Robbie *is holding her arm tightly.*

Daphne   Do you want a new producer?
It's not your decision of course, but –

Robbie   No. It's not going to be as simple as that. (*He looks at her, holding her close, his tone quiet, sharp.*) In the present circumstances, maybe the devil you know is better . . .

Arnos *enters, his manner very avuncular.*

Arnos   I detect a certain edginess, no need for that! The energy from the broadcast still thumping, is it?!

Daphne   I must apologise for what happened, the whole tone was wrong, it got out of hand –

Arnos   No, no apologies are called for. In fact NRD thoroughly enjoyed himself, rather surprisingly!
I have to tell you, my hair stood on end once or twice, I caught myself thinking is this really going out on the British Broadcasting Corporation . . . but people took it as some crazy Marx Brothers episode, didn't they . . . !

Robbie (*surprised*)   They did?

Arnos Oh yes, harmless high spirits, a bite in the trouser leg. Not to be taken literally!
All that talk of secret assignations and forbidden love affairs – it just swam right past them.
There's a real hunger, isn't there – even among such an audience as tonight – for something less rigid and polite. It may have gone over their heads – but they approved!

Clive *enters with* **Isabel**. *They stand slightly apart.* **Clive**'s *manner is very intense, for the first time in the play he is passionately angry. Initially his tone is tightly controlled.*

Clive *I* didn't approve – I absolutely did *not* . . .

Arnos (*blandly*) Well, we would never have expected that!

Robbie *I* wanted Clive to approve . . .

Clive To have had such an audience listening – most of the country will have tuned in – and with the world on the very edge of an abyss . . . the situation could not be more serious . . .
And what do *we* offer people? We ask them to listen to some ridiculous detective squeaking and strutting –

Arnos It is what people want to hear. They want to escape the present uncertainty – that is why he is so popular.

Robbie It wasn't an everyday sort of show, Clive, surely – there *were* things being expressed in it . . . (*Wanting his approval.*) Weren't there?

Clive I can't believe what you did, Robbie – you really think this is a time for settling private scores, do you?! . . . For talking in code, for little jokes about people's sexuality, to please some of your actor friends, to earn marks with them –

Arnos *I* didn't hear any of those private jokes . . .

Robbie I told you I would do something different and I did.

Clive And it was a pathetic response – you had the

whole machine at your disposal, you were completely in charge of it – that's not something that can last long, you know! – You could have done anything you wanted, and instead you resorted to a piece of self-promotion of the most shameless kind.

Pause, he glances around.

You think you've been tapped on the shoulder by America and you can be a little defiant here, a few rude gestures, before you skip off –

Robbie Isabel, stop this please.

Isabel I can't stop him –

Clive No of course you can't. (*To* **Robbie**.) And in fact you bungled it so badly just now, because you don't know whether to be pleased they accepted you and clapped – or annoyed they completely missed your subversive message. (*Sharp.*) Isn't that right!
You want it every way, don't you, Robbie . . . I don't use the word lightly, but you're guilty of real cowardice.

Robbie (*shocked*) Clive . . .

Daphne Mr Lynn-Thomas – these things are best not done in public.

Clive That is precisely the place to do them.

Robbie (*staring across at him*) I'm just a song and dance man, Clive, trying to do his best –

Clive Oh, come on – that is a wretched answer. You want to be more and you know it – and for a moment you had the imagination to respond to what we were trying to do, but when it got to the point, you refused to connect with the real world – you just couldn't face doing it –

Arnos You cannot preach to people on the wireless, that's never been our way – and you certainly can't use a popular entertainer to camouflage your message –

Clive   I have no intention of preaching – I am trying to
make facts live for the mass of the audience. Using Robbie
is a way of reaching them – it's not ideal – but it's a
proper response to the urgency of the situation. *I'm certainly
not telling them what to think* – I've never believed in that. I'm
not trying to force them to be against appeasing Hitler, I'm
just talking about reporting the truth, so people can make
up their own minds.

Arnos   And plenty of them have. They're already
complaining there's far too much news from abroad.

Clive   I don't believe you find that. You receive two
complaints and that suddenly becomes an official policy.
That's the way it happens.
(*Suddenly with real force.*) It's so close, for God's sake, Europe,
where this is happening – *Europe*, that filthy word – you
know how near it is . . . ?!

Arnos (*furious*)   Don't be ridiculous –

Clive   It's so close – you can almost touch it.
It's not some dark primitive continent a million miles away.
If we could walk across the sea, it would be almost a brisk
stroll to where all this is going on, right this second.
But we behave as if it's taking place in a whole other
galaxy, don't we!
We seem to say to our audience this is absolutely nothing
to do with us.
We are part of Europe – these are our people . . . these are
us.

Daphne   That is not true.

Clive   And we're going to reach out and bring that world
even closer. Oh yes.
I will find the evidence, the evidence you are asking for,
eye-witness accounts of real outrages, it will be irrefutable –
confirmed by *three* different sources. I will go and find it
personally, and nothing is going to stop that.
(*Looking at* **Arnos**.) No sinister bureaucratic figure like you,
Mr Grove, is going to stop it . . . always looking over his

shoulder – 'Is somebody after me? Is somebody going to get me?!' Well, there is somebody after you – I'm after you.

Robbie (*jumping up*)   Stop this, Clive – you're destroying all your chances . . . (*Looking at* **Daphne** *and* **Isabel**.) Stop this please – (*He moves.*) this man is not doing himself justice!

Clive   I am going to do this – I will bring the evidence back, and it *will* be broadcast for all to hear. (*He is moving backwards and forwards.*) I'll terrify my way back into the building if necessary in order to achieve it. I will. As you will see. (*He exits.*)

Arnos   That's a wild, wild man.

Isabel   Don't all look at me . . . I have no more control over him, than any of you do.

Arnos   He is a man completely obsessed by his own self-righteousness, isn't he. They are always the most dangerous types.

Robbie (*quiet, looking across at* **Arnos**)   Is that what he is . . .

Arnos   Oh yes. (*To* **Isabel**.) Forgive me, but these things have to be said. He is the sort of character that could only exist in this organisation – with his total lack of practical experience, and possessing absolutely no sense of proportion whatsoever.
Put him in the real world – the place he's fond of talking about – and he'll be torn to shreds within minutes. As we'll see if he goes to Europe. (*He moves to radio in wall.*)

Robbie (*quiet*)   I *wish* you could have stopped him, Isabel.

Daphne   Well, I have to go and type up these notes about what happened today – then I will show them all to you, Robbie, if you can face reading them . . . before they go higher. (*She exits.*)

Dance music is pouring out of the radio.

Arnos Listen – listen to that! Does that sound like a world about to erupt . . .
I ask you, *does it*?!

He moves over to **Robbie**.

You're an admirable chap, Robbie . . . splendidly sensible! You did well to turn the other cheek just now. Have a good break – you deserve it. (*Confidentially*.) We've heard the last of Mr Lynn-Thomas. (*He exits*.)

Robbie *and* **Isabel** *alone*.

Robbie You don't seem worried? Have we heard the last of Clive?

Isabel Oh no . . . I don't think so . . . it won't be as simple as that.

Robbie He insults me . . . he may have ruined his career here . . . he calls me a coward . . . (*Slight pause*.) and yet I feel a burning desire to please him! . . . Isn't that odd? . . . (*He looks across at* **Isabel**.) And apparently I'm a splendidly sensible chap.

Isabel Of course you are.

Robbie And so are you.

Isabel I'm afraid not.

Robbie (*grins*) But splendidly sensible people can be dangerous! . . . and we can . . .

He looks at her.

You'll be my guide, Isabel? Won't you?

Isabel I'm not your guide. I'm not anybody's guide.

Robbie I need a guide . . . always have done – a mentor. And you always know what to do – you don't hesitate . . . you give me energy, you know.

Isabel I give *you* energy – that can't be right.

Robbie You do!

Isabel   I have one or two things of my own to work out, Robbie.

For a moment **Robbie** *sits, singing, half-heard, thoughtfully to himself.*

Robbie *(moving suddenly)*   There's something awful about Arnos's complacency, isn't there! He doesn't think I mind – he's too stupid to see that. (*He stops, self-mocking grin.*) I have to save Clive – further my career, of course! – address the world – outwit Daphne – and hurt Arnos...!

He turns.

Clive's right – I can do anything now ...

The **Assistant** *enters.*

Assistant   Mr Grove would just like to let you know, there's a car and a driver waiting for you when you're ready.

Isabel   A car and a driver – that's a subtle touch, isn't it!

Assistant   There's no hurry ... (*As* **Robbie** *is collecting his shoes.*) Shall I tell you something interesting, Mr Penacourt –

Robbie *(disbelieving)*   You can tell me something *interesting* – can you?!

Assistant   They are thrilled with you, thrilled – you know that. But the real reason for this is, they were so afraid of the commercial stations in Europe – from Luxembourg especially. They pretended they weren't concerned at all – but in fact they didn't know how to fight them ... till you came along! The home audience were leaving them for more exciting variety and music ... but now *you're here.*

Isabel   You're their secret weapon, Robbie ...!

Robbie   Against the commercial wireless from Luxembourg! Now that is quite interesting ...

Assistant   I told you so ...!
When you're ready Mr Penacourt – I'll take you down to your car.

(*As they move.*) I hear Mr Lynn-Thomas is in a spot of bother – is there anything in that? He was always a bit highly strung, wasn't he, rather unconventional.
I always knew to take his advice with a pinch of salt.

Blackout.

Scene Five

Southampton.

The dance music continues for a moment, then breaks into a fragment of one of Neville Chamberlain's Munich broadcasts.

Voice-over 'Yesterday afternoon I had a long talk with Herr Hitler, but it was a friendly one, it was a frank talk but I sincerely feel that one understands what is in the mind of the other ... Perhaps in a few days I'm going to have another talk with Herr Hitler and this time he has told me it is his intention to meet me half way ... he wishes to spare an old man such a long journey ...'

The dance music then comes back for a few seconds, and then we suddenly hear loud and abrupt, a snatch of Orson Welles's radio programme, 'The War of the Worlds'.

'We interrupt this programme to bring you reports of a major incident ...' *etc.*

This in turn gives way to the sound of ships, Tannoy announcements about boarding times for the ships to Antwerp, the sound of rain, and of many voices, a crowd queuing, babies crying, shouts and calls ... the sense of a mass of people very close.

During this final sound section, the lights have come up on **Robbie** *who is on the phone, which is set on the wall. He is shouting through the noise and pressing himself close to the phone.*

Isabel *is standing upstage, smoking.* **Daphne** *is sitting with her large ledger,* **Bernard** *is standing centre stage with passports shuffling and reshuffling his papers.*

Robbie (*calling loudly down the phone*)   Can you hear me,

Solly – (*He calls louder.*) No, no I'm shouting already ... was that better? ... No I can hear *you* ...

Bernard   It's good it's raining, it should be raining for goodbyes. (*He smiles.*) It is almost the official weather for all goodbyes.

Robbie   No, Solly, I can't do anything about the noise, no you don't understand it's *real* ... yes...! It's ships and things, lots of people ... I'm at Southampton ... Yes, boats ... that's right ... no, I've got out of the studio for once ... (*He laughs.*) That's why I can't turn it off!

He looks across at **Daphne**.

No, no, Solly, I was just ringing to make sure Charlie Laughton had got the message to come on the show ... he hasn't?! ... Well, make sure he gets it today ... He's coming into the office ... ? Excellent!
No, I'm planning a really big show for my return from my summer break, yes, everyone in London wants to be on it ... You heard that too?! Terrific!

Bernard   Papers always make me nervous ... passports, visas ... can't help worrying I will forget one ...

Bernard *glances across at* **Robbie** *impatiently, shuffling papers furiously.*

Robbie (*continues on the phone*)   Good, I'm glad you enjoyed the Inspector ... the impact has been quite extraordinary. Yes, *so* make sure Charlie rings me (*He laughs.*) He can meet my new friend Mr Disney ... No he's very agreeable, a very nice man.
Daphne is making signs, yes – she's here of course, she's always with me.

Daphne   Make sure he tells you who's really firm.

Robbie (*into phone*)   Daphne wants to know who's really definite. But I know all of Solly's clients will be definite.

Bernard (*suddenly exasperated*)   How can he be on the telephone at a time like this?

Robbie   Got to go, Solly ... Yes, I'm afraid so – got
many other people to ring. Ring me right back as soon as
there's any news, I'm on Southampton 439. Bye, Solly.

He turns.

Here I am. You must think what an insensitive fellow ...
on the phone ... saying 'no those ships are real, I can't
turn them off!'

Bernard (*sharp grin*)   I'm used to it by now. But it's
important we get all this paperwork right, Robbie.

Robbie   They'll be no problems. You're just going to see
your family ... And you come back as a fellow scriptwriter,
co-creator of Curioso! I have it in writing – it has a
splendid ring to it, 'co-creator'.

Bernard (*to* **Daphne**)   You know he jokes my mother
can come as a senior creative collaborator, and my father
as well, as director of creative collaborators.
I can get my whole family here working on the broadcasts!

Daphne (*quiet*)   Robbie, you shouldn't make jokes like that
... But why ... ?

Bernard   It's all right, I don't take him seriously! I am
the Baron Freiher von Brandis, after all. Come on, let's do
it. I don't mind this part – going out – it's just coming
back, and in Germany too, of course, they study your
papers like they're some ancient manuscript –

Robbie *and* **Bernard** *move to exit.*

Robbie   Don't worry, I will explain everything to the
official, that you're coming back almost immediately for
'The Show of Shows' – (*Broad smile.*) Hopefully all the
border guards will have been listening to my broadcasts!
(*They exit.*)

Daphne (*staring after them*)   Robbie wants me with him all
the time, hardly lets me out of his sight – but it's not an
efficient use of time.

Isabel (*sharp smile*)   An efficient use of time, it's hard to get that right, isn't it – specially when you're saying goodbye. (*She glances towards the noises.*) I've been watching ... so many different ways people find of saying goodbye ... with a little peck of a kiss, or a passionate embrace ... or just a link of the fingers.

Can you tell the strength of a goodbye just by watching from the outside?

Daphne People who really mean it, don't play it out in public.

Isabel Is that right, Daphne? You don't like emotions displayed, do you, messy, people going off in all directions.

Daphne It doesn't embarrass me if that's what you're trying to imply. I'm not as strait-laced as you think.

Isabel But you don't approve of *me*, do you?

Daphne Why do you say that?

Isabel You don't need to be Inspector Curioso to work that out! You think I'm vague, flighty, probably amoral. Somebody who is definitely *not* to be relied on. Why am I here now for instance – except to cause trouble.

Daphne Whenever I think of you, Isabel – I only think of you in relation to Robbie.

Isabel You mean have we been lovers ... ?

Daphne I didn't mean that –

Isabel But you'd like to know! It's not an easy answer, because we had one tangled night, a mixture of hugs and sex. And before you ask – do I sleep with anyone? – No I don't. I love Clive ... I needed comfort that night.

Daphne I wasn't referring to that ... I meant you deflecting Robbie away from his normal work.

Isabel You're very loyal to him, aren't you?

Daphne No that is not true – I'm loyal to my *employers*. I make no secret about that.

I've spent my whole life striving for recognition – that's

how I became one of the first women producers. I'm loyal
to Robbie as long as he's loyal to the Corporation.

Isabel   And *is* he being?

Daphne   We will see. We're both keeping each other
under surveillance as it were . . . I *think* he will be sensible,
but he could go the other way.

Sound of crying and women calling.

Isabel   Something terrible about people queuing, isn't
there – when you can feel their need.

Daphne   People exaggerate their distress to try to stay.

Isabel (*it suddenly snaps out of her*)   You mean *foreigners*
exaggerate?

Daphne   There is no need to get aggressive.
Yes some exaggerate, undoubtedly.
You know I think you mind, Isabel, about how I regard
you, but I can promise you I don't care at all about how
you regard me. And the reason is simple – I don't think
you have the *faintest idea* what real people think.

Isabel   You forget I spend all my time watching 'real
people'.

Daphne   Of course I know how you spend your time, but
that is all rubbish, because you merely select what you
want to use, to confirm your prejudice.
I can tell you people – and I don't use that terrible word
the masses – people can't connect with abroad.
You think a girl like Susan, for instance, from our
broadcasts, you think *she* cares about what happens abroad!
And *yes* the position there is overstated. The Jews are
always exaggerating, painting lurid pictures, we know that
to be the case.
It's not that bad.

Sounds of people.

I think Robbie has dragged me here today partly to try
and affect me.

Isabel   But you remain resolutely unmoved . . . ?

Daphne   No – of course seeing all these people here is
upsetting. Little girls crying and everything – but one has
to remain objective.
We cannot police the world and what's more we have no
moral right to do so.
I was extremely pleased by what's happened – this Munich
settlement. There was a danger of us succumbing to hasty
emotions, about far away places, needlessly endangering our
listeners' lives –

Isabel   And what about other people's lives, the Czechs,
the Jews –

Daphne   I'm talking about this country! I *told* you we
can't do anything about unfortunates abroad.
The most powerful feeling on earth is the desire to protect
your family, your home, people hate, really hate anything
that threatens that – with a force that would stun you,
Isabel.
They would hate those people out there now – if they
threatened.
If you don't understand that, you really don't understand
how people work.
I have no children and yet I understand. I do not patronise
our listeners, I do not sentimentalise them . . . I don't try to
wish them into what they are not.

Isabel   You just know them?

Daphne   Yes.

Isabel (*quiet, but very sharp*)   I wish I had your certainty,
Daphne . . .

Robbie *and* **Bernard** *enter.*

Robbie   I think we made them see sense – cleared all the
paperwork!

Bernard   You feel with all border guards, even with
something very simple like explaining your going to see
your family and coming back in few days – it becomes an

episode in a major spy drama! 'Where has he hidden the
secret documents . . . has he got them inside his tie? . . .'

Robbie (*to* **Daphne**)   Has Solly phoned back about
Charlie Laughton, and Chevalier?

Daphne   No – he won't be responding that quickly.

Robbie   He will – we're going to get all Solly's stars for
'The Show of Shows'.
We've already got a fairly amazing list, haven't we,
Daphne? – including the Silver Minstrels, at last!

He suddenly looks round.

Oh, I think I left my notebook, you know the little green
one. (*He looks straight at* **Daphne**.)
You couldn't go and get it, Daphne . . . because obviously I
have so little time left with Bernard, And there are such
queues out there . . . it'll be at the desk under the big G.

Daphne (*sharp*)   Yes, I'll get it, Robbie (*Moving slowly.*) I'll
go right away.

Robbie   Thank you. (*Pointed.*) You're taking *your* notebook
with you, Daphne?

Daphne   Yes, I thought I might as well try and keep
everything together.

Robbie   Everything together . . . (*Their eyes meet as*
Daphne *passes him.*) If we lose Daphne's notebook, the
whole thing comes tumbling down, isn't that right?!

Daphne (*sharp*)   I'll go and try to find what you've lost,
Robbie. (*She exits.*)

Robbie   I just had to manoeuvre her out of here for a
moment.

Isabel (*staring after* **Daphne**)   Thought it would do her
good, did you, to fight through rivers of people . . . to make
her stand in a queue with them?
I almost want to follow her, and see what happens.

Robbie *faces them.*

Robbie   Now, before you say anything – about how crass I'm being, with Solly and everything, it's not what it seems!

Bernard (*smiling teasingly*)   What's 'not what it seems', Robbie? – Is this the beginning of a Curioso mystery?!

Robbie   Something unbelievable has occurred – a blinding flash of light . . . in every sense . . .

He moves.

You know what happened in the United States three nights ago? This amazing radio broadcast that has panicked America . . .

Isabel   You mean something about Martians?

Robbie   Yes! Mr Orson Welles and his version of 'The War of the Worlds' . . . and people took it *seriously*, and they were fleeing from their houses, climbing into their cars – driving like crazy to escape . . . towards the sea!

Bernard   Oh, the Americans will believe anything.

Robbie   No, no, that's not what it shows.
It's the most gigantic, vivid, whatever mammoth word you want to use – demonstration of the power of the wireless! – the fact that everybody is listening to this one machine –

Isabel   And you can terrify them out of their wits with it?

Robbie   Yes, but if you can terrify them into hurtling into their cars because of an Invasion from Space . . .
Then you can frighten and involve them with what's happening in Europe.
You can make the whole world feel they're there on the streets of German cities . . . experiencing what the Jews are experiencing . . .
(*He mimics.*) 'We interrupt this programme . . . !'
Don't you realise!
I finally saw – so clearly, why Clive wanted to use me – I had never fully understood before. I mean I got the idea . . . but I hadn't realised inside me – till now!
Like always – despite everything, despite his manner . . .

Clive is *ahead* of events!

Bernard Yes, he is.

Isabel I wish he'd come back – I fear for what's going to happen to him over there.

Robbie Yes, Clive, come back! . . . We need you! We should send messages for him . . . over the BBC.

Isabel (*moving*) I feel I'm representing him here . . . (*Slight smile.*) and that doesn't come naturally to me

Robbie But don't you see, both of you, what the plan is now?! I'm going to do this 'Show of Shows', getting every star in town to appear, using the position I've got at the moment . . . they are already all agreeing . . .
And then we – (*He mimics.*) 'We interrupt this programme . . .' Just like 'The War of the Worlds' . . . They are all singing and suddenly we go out on to the streets of a German city . . . without warning we take the audience with us . . . we show them what is really happening . . . We will deliver a wireless experience which will be impossible to ignore.

He smiles.

And you're going to be back for it, Bernard.

Bernard I think so . . . Yes. (*He glances over his shoulder.*) It's very close now to the time I have to leave.

Isabel (*moving to exit*) You need a moment to yourselves.

Robbie Yes, Isabel, thank you.

Isabel I'll go and find how far Daphne has pushed herself into the centre of the queue. (*She exits.*)

Bernard *and* **Robbie** *alone.*

Bernard This time is not goodbye – even though I am going – because I will be back.

Robbie You will be back in five days. Absolutely. I'll be counting.

Bernard   And I will come back as myself. I will drop the Baron Freiher von Brandis. I will kill him off just like you did Inspector Bonnington.
I will face this new country for the first time being myself. Bernard Bernstein. I don't know why I ever entered into the pretence to begin with.

Robbie   Maybe we should all be made to leave and come back. Re-enter as new people. Better people.

Bernard   Don't worry about being better, Robbie – just do your plan.

Robbie   Why do you say it like that? We will do it *together*. You will have *returned*.

Bernard   Of course . . . Just in case I get delayed.

Robbie   Don't worry about the papers – everything's been cleared. And if you have any trouble at the German end – just get me on the phone, OK?
(*He holds him close.*) I miss you already.

Blackout.

Scene Six

Alexandra Palace.

A short news item: 'Herr Hitler himself will henceforth take supreme command of the armed forces. Field Marshal von Blomberg is no longer to be Minister of War or Commander in Chief of the Armed Forces.'

The lights come up on Alexandra Palace. **Isabel** *standing centre stage and* **Honker** *scurrying around her, busying himself, like the first time we met them.*

Isabel   No more rhino droppings? . . . No more of those tropical feathers scattered everywhere?

Honker   No! Just this awful smell of cabbage from the canteen.

Isabel (*laughs*)   The circus has moved on, has it!

Honker   Everything's changing, isn't it . . . And changing so fast.

A phone begins to ring persistently in the distance.

Dredge *and the* **Dancing Girls** *enter, and* **Mabs**. *He is dressed in a general's uniform. The women are in their everyday clothes.*

Honker   There you are. You look . . . you look . . . –

Dredge   Marvellous?

Honker   Yes, well, why not – you do look marvellous.

Dredge   These are our own clothes – but we don't know what we're going to do in them! First time we're going to be seen *ever* – and we don't know what's going to be happening.

Mabs   Robbie is being mysterious . . . I thought I was doing Sergeant Ostler! It was going to be the first time Curioso and Ostler were seen in *the flesh* – but now instead he wants me to be in a general's uniform – it's most disappointing . . .

Honker   I think we're doing some songs and a little comedy stuff about the army. But Mr Penacourt has been on the phone all the time today – it must be important . . .

Dredge (*impatient*)   Let's go and find him then. Maybe there's some notes in the dressing room – he's really got to tell us what's happening!

Mabs, **Dredge** *and the* **Dancing Girls** *exit.*

Honker (*as they leave*)   It'll all come together . . . (*He turns back to* **Isabel**.) You know if by any chance there is a war –

Isabel   There won't be a war.

Honker   No I know – but if there is – you know they're going to shut down this place immediately, it's one of the first things they've got planned.

We have the technology, to get pictures to people, but it will be just an empty space here.

Everybody is too busy for us at the moment, except you.

Isabel   I've always liked being here –

Honker   And if unfortunately war comes – I'm going to enlist straight away! (**Isabel** *turns, watching him closely.*) Because it'll be marvellous to get in there without any waiting around – go after them at once, smash the Bosch, and get it all over.

Isabel   You're going to rush right in there, Honker? Are you?

Honker   Yes. Absolutely!

Isabel   'Absolutely' – Oh, Honker . . . ! (*She moves.*)

Robbie *enters.*

Honker   There you are! There's so much to do, isn't there?

Robbie (*very preoccupied*)   Yes – there are a lot of extraordinary rumours flying about . . . about things happening at Broadcasting House.

Daphne is really busy taking all the calls – she is going to phone me back with the latest developments. (*To* **Honker**.) And what's more, there's something very odd going on *here* too – because I just heard Arnos is marauding around the place.

Honker   I know! I know! First time he has ever been here. Forgive me mentioning this, but Mabs and the others want to talk to you about what's planned. And the musicians are waiting.

Robbie   I will see to all of that, don't worry.

(*To* **Isabel**, *lowering his voice slightly.*) Apparently the management have started complaining – it's like delayed shock after all these weeks – about how skimpily the girls were dressed during the 'All under one Roof' show, and the fact that I was not in a dinner jacket . . . and plugged my *own* song. These were 'unpredictable elements' . . . as they call it.

Isabel (*laughs*)   I don't believe it – the world's on the edge, and *they're* fighting about the fact that you weren't in a dinner jacket for one show!

We hear **Clive**'s *voice in the passage, 'No, no, I know the way thank you.'*

Robbie (*turning moving excitedly*)   He's here, he's arrived!

Clive *enters. He is in an elegant suit. He looks poised, confident. A complete contrast to the crumpled furious figure he was before he went to Germany. He is carrying a small box.*

Robbie   There you are . . . Clive!

Isabel   Darling – are you all right? (*She touches him.*) You certainly look all right . . .

Clive   Hello, everyone. I'm fine. Yes . . .

Robbie   You look terrific . . . Just like the first time I saw you, doesn't he?! Have you just got back?

Clive   No I've been back a couple of days.
You thought I'd return having been knocked about a bit didn't you? Having been given a beating or two, a hunched figure –

Robbie   Covered in bruises yes. Three black eyes!

Isabel   We've been worried about you . . .

Clive   No. It's strange . . . despite the things I've seen – in fact maybe because of them – I feel such incredible energy. I have here (*Indicating box.*) the recordings I went to make. Two families in particular, telling us what's happened to their father, their husband, and their uncle. They tell it with such force, such clarity – they're really moving witnesses. (*Holding the box.*) I've been carrying this around with me like I've been smuggling diamonds.

Robbie   Let me hold it, let me feel it. (*Taking box.*) It's all in there . . .

Honker   We should hear them as soon as possible.

Clive   I got back to read your huge memo, Robbie, about the 'Show of Shows' . . . 'We interrupt this programme to take you over to the streets of Germany'.
That is a tremendous plan – a superb notion.

Robbie   You approve?! That's good, that's really good.

Clive   Yes . . . (*He moves.*) I just have not been able to keep still since I've arrived back, been striding around the place, on the streets, like a madman – even more of a madman than usual! . . .
You remember your amazing debut, Robbie, describing the Crystal Palace fire lighting up the whole city?

Robbie   My first time ever without a script!

Clive   Yes, it's been the complete opposite experience for me – coming back here I've felt *such* a blanket of ignorance over the whole town, people in a fog, so uninformed. I was seized by the urge to start breaking it down physically, right away. I found myself bursting into long speeches to total strangers, people queuing for taxis, I moved along the side of a cinema queue, like a busker, telling them what was happening abroad! What I'd seen!
A completely futile exercise, of course – I just had to let it come out.
(*Moving.*) But all those people *will* respond – when it's presented to them properly . . .

Robbie (*suddenly quiet*)   I haven't heard anything from Bernard. He should have come back by now. But there's not been a word . . .

Arnos *enters.*

Arnos   Here you are . . . my favourite gathering.

Honker (*getting up*)   Mr Grove . . .

Clive   I have returned, as you can see, and you didn't think I would, did you?

Arnos   Why should I care now.

Robbie   What do you mean?

Arnos   Haven't you heard? I am in exile.
NRD has been given my position – the post has been split
in two, but I was offered neither part. Instead I have been
asked to preside over this place ... to keep it out of
trouble ... and to be ready to shut it down in time of war.
Meanwhile Mr Disney has leased us some cartoons ...

Clive   So you've been moved sideways, Arnos!

Arnos   Yes – not part of the inner circle. We always
believe we can be part of the inner circle, don't we, and
when you get there you think nobody can move you out of
it now – not just like that. But it happens!
There have been the most outrageous squabbles, 'Why did
he get such a good seat at the Lord Mayor's Banquet –
why have you been invited to that Royal function and not
I ... ?'
While you've been on your journey, Clive, that's what's
been happening here.

Clive   And very soon you will hear the fruits of that
journey.

Arnos   I'll be interested to see how that is going to
happen.

Clive   You will certainly notice it, I promise you.

Arnos   Really? *Abroad* is difficult – remember. And it
always will be.

Mabs, **Dredge** *and the* **Dancing Girls** *appear.*

Arnos   You're *all* here! It'll be your last visit, so make the
most of it.
I'm introducing a change of diet here – Mr Disney's
cartoons, Milly Dews singing, her own show. No more
members of the public!

He begins to move to exit.

The outlets of broadcasting are changing – it is progress, so people tell me. But my progress is all the wrong way. Been sent to wander the passages, of this ridiculous outfit.

Robbie   Never mind, Mr Grove – we will dedicate our 'Show of Shows' to you.

Arnos (*looks across at him*)   You think you will bring that off, do you? (*He exits.*)

Clive   What did he mean by that?

Honker   Oh, he's giving me Mickey Mouse! All the freedom I've had here . . . those days are over.

Robbie   Cartoons and Milly singing!

Honker *looks at* **Clive**.

Honker   What pictures your journey would make, Mr Lynn-Thomas . . . What you've brought back . . . If one could turn it into pictures!

Clive   That's right . . .

Suddenly glancing at **Mabs** *and the* **Dancing Girls**.

But we could.

Robbie   Of course! Yes! (*Moving.*) We could use Mabs and the girls!

Dredge (*eager to know*)   Use us? How?

Clive   Get on the ground, Mabs.

Mabs   On the ground?

Robbie   Get on your knees, (*Reassuring him.*) it's all right . . . take off your uniform, your jacket.

Clive   And the girls, with their hair tied back, seeing this happen –

Mabs   On my knees? I am a general no more . . . Is that right . . . ?

Clive   You are an old man being beaten.

Mabs   An old Jewish man?

Robbie   Yes. And his daughters watching.

Isabel (*quiet*)   Does it have to be his daughters?

Robbie   You see somebody come up and pull his shirt off, and they kick the old man.

Mabs *is undoing his shirt, taking his shirt off.*

Robbie   An old Jewish man being beaten to death, on the pavement . . . in front of us – right there –

Clive   Coming into people's living-rooms, straight towards them, they see that happen, it would stun them.

Robbie   We can show it now –

Mabs (*on all fours*)   And I lift my head and I cry, and I yell –

Dredge   The girls are screaming – and they're fighting.

Robbie (*quiet*)   You try to fight back but the savagery that these people display –

We see **Robbie** *and* **Clive** *mime beating and kicking* **Mabs** *savagely.* **Mabs** *joining in, crying out expressively. For a moment we see the whole thing visually, with the girls shouting, and* **Mabs** *moving like a blinded man on the floor, getting more and more hurt.*

Honker (*passionately*)   We can show this. We can do this now. It would affect people!

Dredge   And the man's daughters are trying to fight them off.

Robbie   But they are held back and *made* to watch what happens.

Isabel   You couldn't show that.

Robbie (*speeding with thoughts*)   No we couldn't – I don't think we could show *that* – but even little things will touch them, the audience in the living-room.

He moves.

Get up, Mabs, come on, get up, like he's walking along,
Mabs, before it happens, and people just feel they can walk
into him, just barge into him as they pass, because he's
Jewish.

He walks into **Mabs** *hitting him with his shoulder.*

Just so casual, just like that – normal people doing that, in
a way they would never have dreamed of doing before

Clive (*startled, impressed*)   How do you know that, Robbie?
How do you know they do that? – you've never been
there!
You do have an extraordinary instinct . . .

Robbie   We make an effective team, don't we, a real
team!

He stops, his tone changes.

Of course, we can only do what we want here today,
because so few people have televisions . . . The *one* place we
can show them – and they're not watching.

The phone rings. **Honker** *moves towards it.*

Honker . . . no please . . . I think that will be for me. (*He
moves towards it.*) Isabel – do you think you can answer it?
Just say, for the moment you can't find me.

Isabel (*startled*)   Can't find you? (*Takes phone.*) Daphne? . . .
No, Robbie's not here . . . can I find him . . . ? I don't
know if I can find him . . . (*Looks at* **Robbie**, *then to*
Daphne.) You have another phone ringing? Take it . . .
yes I'll hold on.

Clive   I'm going to tell the girls and Mabs more of what's
in the recording . . . Shall I do that, Robbie? . . . Beginning
to form some sort of structure . . . for what we could do?

Robbie (*quiet*)   Yes, you do that.

Clive, *the girls and* **Mabs** *exit.*

Honker   Marvellous is certainly not the right word – but
this is a very good way to hand over to Arnos. A very

good way to leave things. (*He exits.*)

Isabel (*holding phone*)   Robbie, what is this about?

Robbie   People are cancelling, they've heard I'm under a cloud ... they're pulling out of 'The Show of Shows'.
If they can't get hold of me – it makes it a little more difficult for them.
But with each one that cancels, the more threatened the enterprise becomes.

Isabel   Is this because of Daphne? Has she done all this?

Robbie   No, I don't believe so. In fact she's fighting hard to keep it afloat – her professionalism is strong, even if she suspects I'm going to highjack the show.

No I believe this is to do with something much bigger – there's a lot of movement in all the broadcasting world. They've suddenly woken up to the power of what they've got.
Mr Disney for instance won't return my calls now, he's much more interested in negotiating a general deal with the Corporation.
And I think the high-ups have cottoned on that I may be a bit of a risk to this new world, too unpredictable. They want to rein me back.

He stops.

Those girls' faces, Isabel, did you see them just now? the real force of it? If we could project them somehow into people's minds, during 'The Show of Shows'!

Isabel   What would it achieve, Robbie? Finally, what difference would it make?

Robbie (*startled*)   Isabel, I can't believe you're asking that question. You always said we should broadcast the cries, the pain that's happening.

Isabel   And would anyone notice ... ? Is Daphne right about people – or is Clive? I just don't know any more ... (*Into phone.*) Daphne ... ? No I can't find Robbie ... the

Silver Minstrels have cancelled? ... The Butterfly Quartet
have pulled out too ... ? You're still waiting to hear about
the Cream Toffs ... ? Your other phone's ringing ... I'll
hold. (*She smiles.*) I'm not going anywhere.

Robbie   We boast we're bringing the show that shrinks
the globe ... (*He sings for a second.*) The world is small – but
in fact it is me that is getting smaller. (*He moves, sings a
fragment and stops.*)
My power is going, it is slipping away. With each
cancellation it slips a little bit more.

Isabel (*quiet*)   I just can't bear it, Robbie

Robbie   You can't bear what? About the show?

Isabel   No, it's not about the show ...
(*Her mood is intense, but matter-of-fact.*) I just can't bear it all
happening again.
Watching Honker getting ready to rush off to war ... like
my brothers did ...
I can't believe it's all happening again, so soon.
I lose my brothers. I lose my father, because of their
deaths, he is broken ... he never really spoke to anyone
again. Everybody I knew lost their brothers ...
I can't watch that any more.
(*Into phone.*) Yes, I'm still here, Daphne ... there's a
possibility that the Cream Toffs are still on? ... Right,
Milly Dews will only take part if assured the script will be
firmly stuck to ... she wants that in writing! ... I'll tell
him. You want me to hold on ... I can hear another
phone ...

She looks up at **Robbie**.

Robbie (*quiet*)   I know you feel that, Isabel ... but we've
got to do this.

Isabel   You know, I was thrilled when Munich happened
– does that make me no different to Daphne?
Of course I believe in what Clive is doing, I'm not a
pacifist, I can't urge people to do that – because Fascism
has to be stopped.

But it's just ... I just don't think I've ever lost my child's-eye view of the whole adult world crumpling up ... those memories ... don't go away.
And having seen that – I've been in a way floating ever since.
And I cannot be here when that is happening again.

Robbie   You take a few weeks' rest, and it won't seem that bad then. It won't.
But I can't agree with you, Isabel, I can't look for a way of escape, I can't follow you.

He takes the phone.

Daphne ... it's me, tell me the worst. Just two left? I can co-compere with James Lomax but I must swear to keep to the script? Or what? I will be blacklisted. Yes. I see ... I'll have to think. I'll let you know.

Clive *enters with* **Dredge** *and the* **Dancing Girls**. *The girls' hair tied back, pale make-up.*

Clive   We managed to play our recording and I was translating it to Susan.

Robbie   Got to go, Daphne. (*He rings off, turns to* **Clive**.)
If we do this now, here, there's no chance at all of me being allowed on the wireless.

Clive   Why?

Robbie   They are taking complete control of my show.

He moves, suddenly passionate.

Oh, Clive, you were right, you were so right!
I had the machine there – I could do anything...! If only I had realised then, when I had the chance ...

Clive   We never realise these things in time – it's only when we lose them ...

Robbie   I don't believe that! I could have realised! I could! If I'd grown a little quicker – just that bit quicker in my understanding, I could have made a difference. I don't know how big, but it would have been something!

If I hadn't gone to that golden wood for instance – that appeasing speech I did when I had the whole of America listening – if I hadn't tried to please so much!
I had so many opportunities.

Clive We've still got the power here – not for long – but we have. If somehow we can get to people all over the country, get televisions distributed by the thousands! It's ridiculous, of course there isn't time. But if we could have screens in public places, a bank of television sets together – so people would congregate, they would look up, and they could see these girls.

The girls staring out.

They could be reciting the words of the witnesses.

Isabel *quiet, withdrawn, centre stage.*

Robbie No. To do it now, here – that would only be a gesture. We must hang on to the power – to reach a lot of people . . . I must get to the wireless.
(*He does hand signals to musicians.*) Boys, this is what we will do tonight . . . it will still be soothing . . . still just pleasant . . .

Dance music starts.

Not going to throw it away yet – not while there's still the slightest chance.

Dance music continues. They exit. The music stops.

The lights change, domestic, intimate. **Isabel**'s room.
Isabel *unrolls a small piece of carpet, centre stage.*
Then she faces us.

Isabel I'm not sure I will manage to be as clear as I should be in this note . . .
It's difficult to tell the truth at any time, and particularly difficult at a moment like this – but I suppose if I am being truthful – my life ended a long time ago really. I've tried hard not to think like that, but that is the case. So I

cannot come with you.
Forgive me – we three did our best. I really do believe
that.

Isabel *lies down on the ground, on the piece of carpet. Her body
still.*
Clive *lets out a cry. He enters, and sits staring at her.*
Robbie *enters a moment later, and stands a little distance from*
Clive. *Silence.*

Clive (*very quiet*)   There you are.

Robbie   Yes ...

Clive *staring at* **Isabel**.

Clive   We had so little time together.
I was so busy recently ... I was so very busy ...
I loved her ...

Robbie (*quiet*)   I was busy too ... (*Pause, looking at* **Isabel**.)
I'm not sure it would have made any difference, Clive ...

Clive (*with passion*)   Yes, of course it would ...
Her sorrow ... I wasn't there ...

Pause.

Robbie   I didn't know what to do ... so Daphne's here
... Do you mind?

Clive   No.

Robbie   She'll know ... She knows what to do.

Daphne *enters. She goes up to* **Isabel**'s *body and kneels beside
her, her manner is intense, humane.*

Daphne   Oh poor girl ... (*Kneels beside her.*) Oh poor
thing. (*She holds her.*) You can still smell her perfume ... Oh
poor, poor thing ...

*The music starts. The 'Friday Night at Eight' music. One red light
flicks on. High above us the* **Assistant** *announces:*

Assistant   'It's time again for "Friday Night at Eight"!
And your first host for the evening is Mr James Lomax!'

We hear an American voice.

Voice-over   'Well it's "Friday Night at Eight" and I'm James Lomax and here are some of the goodies we have in store.'

On stage **Milly Dews** *is standing with* **Robbie**.

Milly   I can't do it – and I *will* not do it. I made my conditions absolutely clear. And now you want to do something else. I said I'd do the tulip song and one other, and if you won't let me, then I'm afraid I'm withdrawing. I've never had to be so unprofessional before – but I will not do this. It's not even proper music. (*As she moves.*) I will not be dragged into these matters . . .
I give concerts abroad, remember! How can I get involved in all of this?! (*She exits.*)

Robbie *does hand gestures*, **Dredge** *comes on.*

Assistant*'s voice*   'And now our co-compere for the evening, Mr Robbie Penacourt.'

Dredge   I think I can do it, Mr Penacourt, I want to do it anyway.

Robbie   Do your best . . . that will be fine . . .
This is the best *I* can do now, Susan.

The other red light flicks on.

This is Robbie Penacourt. I will not be doing the songs that were mentioned by Mr Lomax – nor will I be doing Inspector Curioso.

Instead I am doing a song written by a Jewish man who lived in Munich until very recently.
In a moment I will tell you a little about his life and what has happened to him and his family.

The music starts.

Hearing the song will comfort – because it's a beautiful song – but it's not meant to comfort.

He sings for a moment. Then stops. Quiet, simple.

It will reassure – but I promise you, it shouldn't
reassure . . .

Robbie *starts to sing again.* **Dredge** *accompanies him. They sing together in German.*

Fade.